HUMANITY
COMING OF AGE

Minneapolis

Second Edition June 2024

Humanity Coming of Age: How a united global civilization can emerge from the chrysalis of despair. Copyright © 2024 by Massoud Kazemzadeh and Gary Lindberg. All rights reserved.

No parts of this book may be used or reproduced by any means, graphic, electronic, or mechanical, including photocopying, recording, taping or by any information storage retrieval system, without the written permission of the publisher except in the case of brief quotations embodied in critical articles and reviews.

10 9 8 7 6 5 4 3 2

ISBN: 978-1-962834-17-9

Cover and book design by Gary Lindberg

HUMANITY
COMING OF AGE

How a united global civilization can
emerge from the chrysalis of despair

MASSOUD KAZEMZADEH
GARY LINDBERG

Minneapolis

We desire the good of the world and the happiness of the nations that the bonds of affection and unity between the sons of men should be strengthened... what harm is there in this? ... these fruitless strifes, these ruinous wars shall pass away, and the 'Most Great Peace' shall come.

– Bahá'u'lláh, *Paris Talks*

Table of Contents

Chapter 1: The Soul of Humanity 1
Chapter 2: Disillusionment and Hope 17
Chapter 3: The Oneness of a Diverse Humanity 29
Chapter 4: Sin and Mortality 49
Chapter 5: Science and Religion 73
Chapter 6: Prejudice 85
Chapter 7: Equalilty of Women and Men 101
Chapter 8: Universal Education 125
Chapter 9: Economic Justice 145
Chapter 10: Social Justice and Action 165
Chapter 11: Human Rights 179
Chapter 12: Universal Peace 193
Chapter 13: The Environment 203
Chapter 14: The Prosperity of Humankind 215
Afterword 237
Research and Study Sources 239
Acknowledgements 241
About the Author 242

To all humanity without distinction or conditions

Chapter 1:
The Soul of Humanity

Our first book, *The Soul of Humanity*, is a general appeal to abandon blind faith and apply rational thinking to all important matters of life from science and relationships to politics and religion. That book is a meaningful prerequisite for this one as it provides the framework for making sense out of a cohesive and rational plan for the maturing of humanity. For readers unfamiliar with that book or who would like a quick summary, it suggests that nothing, especially religion, should be exempt from intellectual scrutiny.

In our understanding, the First Law of Thermodynamics as described in *The Soul of Humanity* clarifies scientifically that humanity is of a higher form of organized creation than animals, and that what distinguishes humans from animals is an entity that has been called the rational soul, a function of which is logical thinking. It is this rational soul, which is unique to humans, that gives rise to imagination, logical thinking, and eventually to the advancement of humanity. This unique quality of humans is not of the material world but of a higher existence.

> The human spirit, which distinguishes man from the animal, is the rational soul, and these two terms—the

> human spirit and the rational soul—designate one and the same thing.[1]

The Reality of One God

The Soul of Humanity attempts to build a rational case for the existence of a single God, an indescribable force responsible for the existence of the natural world. The word "God" may be off-putting to some people because of fanciful descriptions of s supreme being that have been offered by countless others. What we mean by God is a Divine Essence or Force that is literally undefinable and far beyond the grasp of human minds. Even the term "One God" does not fully apply any more than if we were to say "one gravity." In one sense, it is true, but in a larger view, even referring to the singleness of an entity such as God seems too limiting.

In humankind's attempts to understand the undefinable, humankind since its creation has invented innumerable stories and humanized myriad personalities and images to help our human minds relate to a Creator that we cannot see or touch. For this reason, in *The Soul of Humanity* we attempted not to explain the Divine but merely to prove that there must be an existence higher than animals, higher even than humans—an existence that imbued each human with a rational soul—the power of rational thought, imagination, insight, understanding of complex material and spiritual concepts—all abilities not possessed by any other creature traditionally categorized in the Animal Kingdom.

> Minerals, plants and animals are bereft of the mental faculties of man that discover the realities of all things, but man himself comprehendeth all the stages beneath him. Every superior stage comprehendeth that which

---

1 'Abdu'l-Bahá, *Some Answered Questions*, Page 208

> is inferior and discovereth the reality thereof, but the inferior one is unaware of that which is superior and cannot comprehend it. Thus man cannot grasp the Essence of Divinity, but can, by his reasoning power, by observation, by his intuitive faculties and the revealing power of his faith, believe in God, discover the bounties of His Grace... The Divine Essence as it is in itself is however beyond all description.[2]

Other concepts such as gravity, the electro-magnetic spectrum, the endless orbiting of atoms around a nucleus, for example—have been proven even though there is no scientific definition for how these phenomena work. We suggest that the same is true of the Divine.

> If you should ask a thousand persons, "What are the proofs of the reality of Divinity?" perhaps not one would be able to answer. If you should ask further, "What proofs have you regarding the essence of God?" "How do you explain inspiration and revelation?" "What are the evidences of conscious intelligence beyond the material universe?" "Can you suggest a plan and method for the betterment of human moralities?" "Can you clearly define and differentiate the world of nature and the world of Divinity?"—you would receive very little real knowledge and enlightenment upon these questions... People speak of Divinity, but the ideas and beliefs they have of Divinity are in reality superstition.[3]

In the end, acceptance of the Divine will always remain personal. Proof of the existence of the Divine must follow a rational path for proof like that of mathematics.

---

2 'Abdu'l-Bahá, *Tablet to August Forel*, Page 16
3 'Abdu'l-Bahá, *The Promulgation of Universal Peace*, p. 326

The Reality of One Unfolding Religion

The Soul of Humanity presents a rational explanation for the sequential appearance of "Prophets" and their Teachings, which have provided the spiritual and ethical foundation for the world's great wisdom traditions often referred to as "religions." Unfortunately, the term "religion" has been so misrepresented and wrongly understood that it has come to mean something that younger generations shun. According to the book's explanation, these successive wisdom traditions revealed a progressive unfoldment of spiritual truths and practical laws, each "revelation" building on the knowledge developed by its predecessors.

If all religions, then, were part of one continuous educational process delivered to different cultures over thousands of years, it seems logical that there is only one religion of God that humankind is discovering incrementally in the same way that we are discovering the laws and principles of science over time. Even if it is not known in its entirety by everyone and has been interpreted and modified by humans in various ways, the core truths of these faiths remain available.

If there is one God known by dissimilar names and understood differently by diverse people, and if there is just one religion that has been revealed in stages but unfortunately corrupted and misinterpreted to serve the selfish interests of humans, where does that leave us? *The Soul of Humanity* proposes that by expanding our spiritual knowledge and modernizing many of the old material laws, each "Prophet" has provided humanity with an updated owner's manual for living well in an ever-advancing society and getting along with others. All we have to do is consult that manual and follow its advice.

> Although the received truths of the great faiths remain valid, the daily experience of an individual in the twenty-first century is unimaginably removed from the one that he or she would have known in any of those ages when this guidance was revealed… [Countless changes]

> affecting every aspect of human life, have brought into being a new world of daily choices for both society and its members. What has not changed is the inescapable requirement of making such choices, whether for better or worse.[4]

Unfortunately, humans usually favor the "Prophet" they already know and persecute those who announce changes to address the needs of a new era. People have such affection for their accepted Prophet they ignore all the previous Prophets and condemn any who follow. Some avid believers go so far as to conflate the Prophet they follow with God, a station of Divinity that none of the Prophets have claimed for Themselves.

Refusing to even consider the claims of a new "Divine Educator" may seem irrational and short-sighted, but this is how devout belief becomes prejudice. And yet we find that each of the Founders of the major wisdom traditions acknowledged their continuous chain of custody of Truth. According to Gautama Buddha:

> I am not the first Buddha who came upon the earth nor shall I be the last. In due time another Buddha will arise in the world, a holy one, a supremely enlightened one, endowed with wisdom in conduct, auspicious, knowing the universe, an incomparable leader of men, a master of angels and mortals. He will reveal to you the same eternal truths, which I have taught you. He will preach his religion, glorious in its origin, glorious at the climax and glorious at the goal. He will proclaim a religious life, wholly perfect and pure such as I now proclaim. His disciples will number many thousands while mine number many hundreds.[5]

---

4   The Universal House of Justice, *One Common Faith*.
5   Gautama Buddha, *Gospel of Buddha by Carus* (Ceylon Sources), pp. 217-218.

According to the Bahá'íBahá'í Writings:

> Every prophet predicted the coming of a successor and every successor acknowledged the Truth of the predecessor. Moses prophesied the coming of Christ. Christ acknowledged Moses. His Highness Christ foretold the appearance of Muhammad, and Muhammad accepted The Christ and Moses. When all these divine prophets were united with each other, why should we disagree?[6]

The perennial proof of God's existence...

> is that from time immemorial He has repeatedly manifested Himself... One is free to dispute through historicist interpretations of the evidence the unique role of this or that Messenger of God, if that is one's purpose, but such speculation is of no help in accounting for developments that have transformed thought and produced changes in human relationships critical to social evolution. At intervals so rare that the known instances can be counted on one's fingers, the Manifestations of God have appeared, have each been explicit as to the authority of His teachings and have each exerted an influence on the advance of civilization incomparably beyond that of any other phenomenon in history.[7]

Nevertheless, many people wonder how there can be a unity of the religions revealed by these Manifestations since each has conflicting laws and doctrines, but we do not speak of the unity of religions as they exist today. All religions have gradually become bound by tradition, dogma and myriad opinions of meaning—all the accretions of which are gathered like barnacles on the hull of the original Teachings, which in some cases are lost.

---

[6] 'Abdu'l-Bahá, *Talks in Paris and London*
[7] The Universal House of Justice, *One Common Faith*.

Regarding conflicting laws, a deeper look into the fundamental verities proposed by each wisdom tradition reveals that they are of two types: spiritual laws and practical or material laws.

> The spiritual part never changes. All the Manifestations of God and His Prophets have taught the same truths and given the same spiritual law. They all teach the one code of morality… The practical part of religion deals with exterior forms and ceremonies, and with modes of punishment for certain offences…

> In the time of Moses, there were ten crimes punishable by death. When Christ came this was changed; the old axiom "an eye for an eye, and a tooth for a tooth" was converted into "Love your enemies, do good to them that hate you," the stern old law being changed into one of love, mercy and forbearance! In the former days the punishment for theft was the cutting off of the right hand; in our time this law could not be so applied. In this age, a man who curses his father is allowed to live, when formerly he would have been put to death. It is therefore evident that whilst the spiritual law never alters, the practical rules must change their application with the necessities of the time.[8]

The concept of "one religion," then, applies only to the original, unchanged teachings of each Divine Educator or Manifestation of God. For older religions, it can be hard to find and verify those original spiritual laws or guidance—many are now lost, so all we have left are teachings revised and interpreted by humans. Scholars who have studied religions comparatively, however, have found that many foundational spiritual principles are often emphasized across various religions. Here are some examples:

---

8   'Abdu'l-Bahá, *Paris Talks*.

1. *Love and Compassion*: Virtually all major religions advocate for the practice of love and compassion toward others. This includes showing kindness, empathy, and care for fellow human beings, as well as extending compassion to all living beings.

2. *Justice and Fairness*: Religions often encourage treating others with fairness, equity, and respect, and upholding moral principles that promote justice and social harmony.

3. *Forgiveness and Mercy*: Many religions teach the importance of forgiveness and mercy toward oneself and others. They promote the idea of letting go of resentment, practicing forgiveness and showing mercy even in the face of wrongdoing.

4. *Truth and Honesty*: These virtues are prized in numerous religious traditions. Religions often encourage adherents to be truthful in their words and actions, promoting integrity and trustworthiness.

5. *Humility and Selflessness*: These spiritual principles are regarded as virtues in many religious teachings. They involve recognizing one's limitations, putting the needs of others before one's own and cultivating a sense of humility in the presence of the Divine.

6. *Service and Generosity*: The act of selfless service and generosity is highly regarded across religions. Such actions include helping those in need, contributing to the welfare of others and practicing charity without expecting anything in return.

7. *Inner Peace and Spiritual Growth*: Religions highly recommend the pursuit of inner peace and spiritual growth. This involves practices such as meditation, prayer, contemplation and self-reflection to cultivate a deeper connection with the Divine and attain spiritual well-being.

8. *Respect for Life and Creation*: Many religions emphasize the sacredness of all life and promote responsible stewardship

of the environment and the natural world. They encourage respect for the Earth and its resources, advocating for sustainable practices and the preservation of the planet.

Some people have suggested that the Golden Rule—treating others the way we want them to treat us—should be sufficient guidance for humanity. What could be more comprehensive and universal? And yet the Golden Rule is inadequate when applied to all the peoples of the world. In certain communities, child brides or female genital mutilation may be acceptable for the betterment of society, so these practices would fall under the Golden Rule. But these local customs today are irrational and even harmful, demonstrating that the Golden Rule as a universal law can be applied unequally and falls apart under some conditions.

The Reality of One Human Family

The Soul of Humanity suggests that a fundamental teaching of all existing wisdom traditions—strongly inferred by the older ones and made abundantly clear in the most recent teachings—is that every individual is a member of one magnificently diverse human family. This oneness of all humanity transcends differences of culture, class, ethnicity, race, customs, opinions or temperaments.

> Know ye not why We created you all from the same dust? That no one should exalt himself over the other. Ponder at all times in your hearts how ye were created. Since We have created you all from one same substance it is incumbent on you to be even as one soul, to walk with the same feet, eat with the same mouth and dwell in the same land, that from your inmost being, by your deeds and actions, the signs of oneness and the essence of detachment may be made manifest.[9]

---

9 Bahá'u'lláh, *The Hidden Words of Bahá'u'lláh*, Part 1 from the Arabic, 68.

> Ye are the fruits of one tree, and the leaves of one branch. Deal ye with one another with the utmost love and harmony, with friendliness and fellowship.[10]

Acceptance that all humanity comes from the same dust is rapidly gaining ground around the world despite fierce resistance from racists and other prejudiced individuals. Increasingly, it is apparent to all thinking people that great minds and profound thoughts arise from people of all races, nationalities and religions. Today, our greatest inventors, scientists, mathematicians and artists comprise by themselves a vibrant multinational and multiracial society.

Rationality and Prejudice

The Soul of Humanity proposed many other conclusions that the authors attempted to justify through rational thinking. We have shown that what misleads humanity from a more productive way of thinking is a commitment to ignorance that can be easily corrected by education, which helps one gain knowledge. If one does not know the science of how rain occurs, old cultural practices of dancing and chanting may seem like reliable catalysts for a shower. But as one learns the science of how rain develops, superstitious rituals disappear. Prejudices are based on a commitment to ignorance we call "blind faith".

- Rational thinking usually reaches incorrect conclusions when the information analyzed is incomplete, distorted inadvertently or on purpose, misunderstood or otherwise flawed. Trusted sources sometimes prove to be untrustworthy. It is up to each individual to seek the most trustworthy information available at the time and do their own rational analysis.

---

10   Bahá'u'lláh, *Gleanings from the Writings of Bahá'u'lláh*

- Science and religion are not competing knowledge systems. Since both are the creation of one God, they must be in harmony with each other. Apparent differences are due to incomplete knowledge of one or the other or misunderstandings derived from false information or unproven theories, even those that are generally accepted.

- Regrettably, religion has often been the cause of disunity and strife, not because the original Teachings were flawed but because they have been so often misinterpreted, hijacked for selfish purposes, tainted by innate human prejudices, and corrupted in countless other ways.

- The lack of universal education, particularly the withholding of education for girls and women in many parts of the world, has contributed to a global society that lacks the knowledge and critical thinking skills needed for solving the world's problems. When education devolves into indoctrination that discourages independent thinking, however, the danger escalates.

- Prejudices, often rooted in blind faith and adherence to meaningless traditions and outdated rituals, is a frequent companion of ignorance. For civilization to advance, all prejudices must be annihilated, including racism, sexism, ageism, cultural and ethnical stereotypes, language and religious biases.

Social Transformation

The three onenesses—one God, one unfolding religion, one human family—are the foundation on which is built a remarkable and rational system for bringing about meaningful social transformation and addressing the frustrating problems faced by humanity today. Exploring this system rationally is the mission of this book.

All religions have come to unite humanity, yet humankind

has misinterpreted the scriptures to divide humanity. The social judgements of people in our communities today are often based on religious affiliation, wealth, race, mental capacity, et cetera. They arose from religious malpractice and must be eliminated. Religion is and always has been a personal commitment, and today, with improved literacy levels, there is little need for religious "authorities" to interpret truth for anyone but themselves.

About This Book

Many readers of *The Soul of Humanity* requested a follow-up volume that would explore whether the spiritual principles presented could help establish the biggest goals of society—the end of wars and the peace and tranquility of all peoples.

This is no small task, but the authors have accepted the challenge and offer this book as a response. We want to be clear, though, that while the principles we will present seem rational to us, you may disagree with our conclusions. The principles themselves were not invented by the authors but rather revealed in the Teachings of the world's most recent wisdom tradition. The truth of each principle should be evaluation, however, not based on its source but on whether it makes sense in today's world. Together, these rational principles comprise a cohesive and actionable plan for bringing about an ever-advancing civilization.

Conventions Used in This Book

Capitalization

Throughout this book, the authors have chosen to capitalize words that refer to the Divine or the Revelation of the Divine, including pronouns. This practice honors the generally accepted conventions followed in many of the sacred Scriptures of the world's great wisdom traditions. Nevertheless, there are capitalization inconsistencies in quoted King James versions of various biblical passages. We have chosen to always use the capitalization originally used in Scriptural passages even when they are fossilized compared to modern usage.

Use of Masculine Gender

Spirits or souls are not of this material world so gender is meaningless when referring to them, and yet we lack suitable pronouns for entities that have no gender. In many languages, the use of the masculine gender, unless intended specifically to denote masculinity, is considered generic or lacking specific gender. For instance, in English we speak of the race of man, or mankind, in both instances meaning every member of the human race—men, women and children. There would be no reason to interpret "O Son of Being", or "O Son of Man" as addressed only to males. It is the same with pronouns.

> The truth is that all mankind are the creatures and servants of one God, and in His estimate all are human. "Man" is a generic term applying to all humanity. The biblical statement "Let us make man in our image, after our likeness" does not mean that woman was not created. The image and likeness of God apply to her as well. In Persian and Arabic there are two distinct words translated into English as man: one meaning man and woman collectively, the other distinguishing man as male from woman the female. The first word and its pronoun are generic, collective; the other is restricted to the male. This is the same in Hebrew.[11]

The problem of commonly used gender-specific nouns (chairman, postman, mankind) has two potential solutions. One is to

---

11 'Abdu'l-Bahá, *The Promulgation of Universal Peace: Talks Delivered by 'Abdu'l-Bahá during His Visit to the United States and Canada in 1912*, rev. ed. (Wilmette: Bahá'í Publishing Trust, 1995), pp. 174 and 374.

change the usage of nouns; the other is to permit the consciousness of sexual equality to modify the meaning of nouns that were once standard usage. Undoubtedly, both courses will be followed in the evolution of the language. The word "doctor," for example, is now clearly of common gender in English, although originally masculine. In specifically addressing this issue, the Bahá'í Faith issued the following statement:

> Our feeling is that, in general, it is preferable to permit the change of consciousness to change the meaning that people attribute to the words, rather than to press the use of forms of words that seem contrived and, to many people, ridiculous—a reaction that does not help the advancement of the cause of the equality of the sexes.[12]

The authors agree with this assessment and have chosen to ask readers of this to interpret masculine pronouns and nouns in quoted passages to explicitly apply to both males and females. In the fresh material written by the authors, however, an attempt has been made to avoid the issue by making inclusive word choices or including both gender-based pronouns. These language issues are not trivial, as language is our chief tool for communication with each other and bringing about the unity of humankind.

Diacritics

A diacritic is a mark near or through a written character or combination of characters indicating a phonetic value different from that given the unmarked or otherwise marked element. We often think of diacritics as accent marks or symbols above or below letters (examples: Ḍ ẓ Á í Gh kh). Bahá'í Writings use a standard system of conventions used for writing a language to

---

[12] November 1989, from a memorandum from the Universal House of Justice to a Bahá'í Office of Public Information.

Romanize Persian and Arabic script. The system used in Bahá'í literature was set in 1923, and although it was based on a commonly used standard of the time, it has its own embellishments that make it unique. The authors have chosen to use Bahá'í diacritics when documenting names or words originating in the Persian or Arabic languages.

Use of Scriptural Passages and Spiritual Principles

Throughout this book, the authors refer to Writings from the world's great wisdom traditions, often considered as world religions. The intent of the authors is for these passages to be considered on their own merits as traditional wisdom, not because they may have been of Divine origin. There is no intent to promote one of these religions over another; in fact, we believe an individual should study them all. The fact that there are a greater number of quotations from the Bahá'í Faith is due to the fact that while older wisdom traditions spoke rationally, they were speaking to less knowledgeable societies that lacked sophisticated scientific knowledge, and thus the older wisdom traditions seldom if ever commented on the modern issues this book addresses. Commentary on religious scriptures in this book express the authors' personal views, which are informed by their study and understanding of Bahá'í Writings.

Chapter 2:
Disillusionment and Hope

Most people today are disillusioned with the state of the world. Despite enormous technological and medical breakthroughs, public discourse seems to have deteriorated, military conflicts continue to disrupt global security, political disputes and corruption plague numerous nations, prejudice and violence have overtaken society, and worsening climate change threatens the life of our planet. Amazingly, some religious groups are still promoting prayer as a means of curing ailments that can be treated by medical therapies. Some even believe their special beliefs indemnify them from real world consequences and eventually God will take them up into the clouds before He destroys all those who disagree with their superior beliefs. It is easy to feel depressed at the present state of affairs.

    A longer view, however, shows that civilization has grudgingly been making glacial progress from its earlier and more primitive states. In fact, we may be living at a very special time in humanity's development, which has passed through various stages similar to infancy and adolescence. Looking at the diorama of human history from a distance, it appears that humankind now stands at the beginning of its maturity. As we know, even adults occasionally relapse into childish behavior and make bad decisions. It is possible that this stage of society's evolution will finally witness the unification of humankind and the blossoming of a richly diverse, more just and tranquil world civilization.

For many, this vision may seem unattainable considering humanity's poor track record, but two inseparable forces are relentlessly propelling us toward maturity. These are the processes of disintegration and integration.

A Two-fold Process of Transformation

At the present time, a two-fold process is at play destined "to bring to a climax the forces that are transforming the face of our planet."[13] The process of destruction and disintegration ...

> ...tends to tear down, with increasing violence, the antiquated barriers that seek to block humanity's progress towards its destined goal [and is identified with] a civilization that has refused to answer to the expectation of a new age, and is consequently falling into chaos and decline.[14]

Simultaneously, a constructive process of integration is also underway, though this process receives far less recognition because it is less dramatic. We can see the results of this process with increased collaboration between nations and broader recognition of the basic human rights and dignity of all people.

Outworn and destructive mindsets are at the heart of the process of disintegration—authoritarianism, racism, ultra-nationalism, religious extremism of all types, patriarchal attitudes, xenophobia, and many other negative influences. Though still stubbornly embraced by some people, these outworn paradigms have been largely exposed and delegitimized. Nevertheless, we continue to witness many angry

---

13 *The World Order of Bahá'u'lláh*, p. 170.
14 *Lights of Guidance*, Bahá'í Publishing Trust

battles by zealous partisans to protect these destructive attitudes. There are so many minor skirmishes that it sometimes seems like the zealots are gaining ground. In fact, however, they may be doing the necessary work of exposing and tearing down the pillars of the old systems so a new mindset can be constructed on the ruins. We are in the middle of this reconstruction. The gradual disappearance of the order of the old world masks the emergence of a new order, a new consciousness, a new way of thinking.

Evidence of the Constructive Process of Integration at Work

Empirical evidence abounds in historical data to support that the constructive process is successfully advancing. Because statistical data changes frequently, we suggest you consult a rich source of such information compiled by Max Roser at www.ourworldindata.org.

More generally, we find that since the mid-nineteenth century, a sharp increase in scientific discoveries and technological innovations has occurred. During this period, we also find increased recognition of human rights and a sharp rise in the number of laws against slavery. These changing mindsets influenced the adoption of the Universal Declaration of Human Rights in 1848, a cornerstone of international law. The Human Rights Index, consisting of life expectancy, literacy, health, education and GDP data, has shown a steady improvement in all categories over the last century.

- Despite the focus on bloody wars and violence in our ravenous 24-hour news cycle, there was a significant decrease in violence and war deaths as of 2017 despite a rise in deaths by firearms in the US. Roya Akhavan, Ph.D., wrote in the 2017 book *Peace for Our Planet: A New Approach*:

> During the nineteenth century, the French Revolutionary Wars killed seventy out of every hundred thousand

> people. In the twentieth century, despite two world wars and a few genocides, the average number of war deaths went down to sixty out of one hundred thousand. So far, in the twenty-first century, the worldwide average of the number of deaths caused by wars is down dramatically to 0.3 per hundred thousand.[15]

In a book published in 2011, David Pinker, a psychology professor at Harvard, summarized other important positive indicators of a decline in violence and a delegitimizing of war and violence internationally[16]:

- The end of the Cold War and tearing down of the Iron Curtain in the early 1990s. The recent invasion of Ukraine by Russia only shows that the road to a more peaceful world is still rocky.
- China's abandonment within two decades of the extreme actions of Mao's Cultural Revolution and its emergence as a trading partner of multiple countries.
- South Africa's abolishment of apartheid—institutionalized racism—and the peaceful transfer of power from its White minority to the Black majority.
- The waning of fascism and dictatorships as democratic nations increased from twenty in 1976 to over 100 today.
- The remarkable development of a multilateral economic collaboration in Europe, which had given the world two of its bloodiest wars. The European Union (EU) currently has its own European Parliament, a body of laws, a European court system and a common currency.
- Arrangements like the EU that have emerged in South America (UNASUR), Southeast Asia (ASEAN) and Africa (AU).

---

15 Roya Akhavan, Ph.D., *Peace for Our Planet: A New Approach*, p. 11.
16 Steven Pinker, *The Better Angels of Our Nature: Why Violence Has Declined*.

- The end of colonialization and the granting of formal independence of all foreign colonies by the 1970s.

Other notable examples known to most of us but often forgotten as indicators of humanity's irrepressible forward march include:

- The birth of the interfaith movement in 1893 when representatives from Christian, Muslim, Jewish, Hindu and Buddhist faith traditions met in Chicago for peaceful and respectful dialogue. A century later, the Parliament of World Religions was formed representing fifty faith traditions in eighty countries.
- The women's suffrage movement—begun four years after a new world religion called the Bahá'í Faith boldly declared in 1844 the spiritual principle of the equality of women and men—eventually won the passage in Congress of the 19th Amendment to the US Constitution guaranteeing women the right to vote.
- The rapid rise of peace societies to nearly 400 organizations from the mid-nineteenth century to the end of it.
- The establishment of a Permanent Court of International Justice and the world's first formally organized international body, the League of Nations. Though the League lasted only two years, it set an important precedent for a more advanced collective system of supranational cooperation, the United Nations (UN.)
- The unprecedented means for civil society to engage with national governments in advancing human rights, global health and economic development through the formation of non-governmental organizations (NGOs).

- The 2015 Paris agreement on preserving the environment—the first pact ever signed by all the sovereign countries in the world.

Evidence of the Destructive Process of Disintegration at Work

The clear indicators of a maturing civilization listed above, along with many others, do not demonstrate that we have arrived at utopia. Each of those achievements is "but a faint glimmer in the darkness that envelops an agitated humanity.[17]" Obviously, we still have a long way to go, and the parallel destructive process of disintegration has been showing remarkable resistance.

- Extremists of many stripes perceive positive change—any change, actually—as an existential threat and retaliate with vengeance or acts of terrorism.
- In the Middle East, religious fundamentalists seek to reestablish caliphates and revive repressive versions of Sharia law.
- In the US, backward-looking opinion leaders and others seek to return society to a nostalgic time of white supremacy, male domination, religious intolerance, immigrant persecution, gender shaming and economic enslavement of people who are "different."
- Around the world, a new crop of strong-man leaders seek to attract the coveted blind faith of ardent followers by promising to turn back the clock to the "good old days" of repression, suppression and oppression of a new majority now made up of a motley bunch of hated minorities.
- Once-feared national leaders of fading nations expose their desperation by threatening or attacking weaker neighbors militarily or economically.

---

17   Shoghi Effendi, *The World Order of Bahá'u'lláh*.

- Corruption in governments and businesses makes the rich richer and the poor poorer; the lack of economic justice is a proven formula for social upheaval.
- Everywhere, grudges for offenses real or imagined are "settled" by force rather than consultation, which establishes new vicious circles of retaliation.

These kinds of misguided mindsets are historic; they have always plagued our world. Unfortunately, we are not at the end of this process of disintegration.

> The process of disintegration must inexorably continue, and its corrosive influence must penetrate deeper and deeper into the very core of a crumbling age.[18]

This dark admonition may seem gloomy, but with deeper reflection it is stunningly logical. The process of disintegration is necessary for the process of integration to go forward because these two processes are parallel. As the constructive process gains critical mass, the destructive process diminishes accordingly. Rather than endlessly repairing our old house, which is collapsing around us, we are watching it fall down as we construct a new house that is more spacious and responsive to the needs of the time.

Historically, we have seen that direct action cannot alone change destructive attitudes and actions. Just as cold is the absence of heat, the antidote for a negative attitude that fuels the destructive process is a more powerful positive attitude.

> When a thought of war comes, oppose it by a stronger thought of peace. A thought of hatred must be destroyed by a more powerful thought of love. Thoughts of war bring destruction to all harmony, well-being, restful-

---

18 Shoghi Effendi, *The World Order of Bahá'u'lláh*.

> ness and content... Thoughts of love are constructive of brotherhood, peace, friendship, and happiness.[19]

Of course, more than positive thoughts are required to accelerate the constructive process, but most actions begin with intent. In other words, action is of two types—instinctive (performed automatically, unconsciously or impulsively without thinking or reasoning) and intentional. Intentional actions always arise from a conscious thought process and are willfully carried out after a deliberate decision to perform them. Not all thinking results in intentional actions, but intentional actions are usually required to bring about significant change, by definition cannot occur without thinking about them first. As the quotation above emphasizes, the nature of those thoughts can have great influence on the resulting actions, which in turn can help achieve desired results. The spiritual principle underlying this truth is that all our constructive actions begin with rational thought.

Accelerating the Constructive Process

As we've seen, two parallel processes are at work in the world simultaneously, one destructive and the other constructive. If we favor a world in which prejudice does not rule, injustices are not permitted and wars are not viewed as sport that devalues and prizes power, it makes sense to support and even accelerate the constructive process. As the constructive process advances, the destructive process necessarily declines, though it may put up a highly visible fight to keep its support from dwindling.

The remainder of this book proposes a rational system for accelerating the constructive process. This system is based on spiritual principles that arise from the world's great wisdom traditions and are independent of partisan politics, which by definition are divisive. These principles can be seen as useful even when considered

---

19 'Abdu'l-Bahá, *Paris Talks*.

separately, but when combined they comprise a systematic approach to bringing about cooperative behavior and an ever-advancing civilization.

Independent Investigation of Reality

A foundational principle is the independent investigation of reality to discover truth. Not found in any sacred Book of the past, this principle, so concisely stated below, has enormous implications for humanity.

> ...every individual member of humankind is exhorted and commanded to set aside superstitious beliefs, traditions and blind imitation of ancestral forms in religion and investigate reality for himself. Inasmuch as the fundamental reality is one, all religions and nations of the world will become one through investigation of reality.[20]

This principle calls each person to open their minds, abolishes the practice of religious coercion and the need for clergy, sets us free from imitating past traditions and blindly adhering to unexamined dogma, and gives each individual the right *and the duty* to search for and decide on their own what they believe. Without this prerequisite principle, searching for truth is futile and the unity of civilization is impossible. It allows all people, after a sincere investigation of reality, to make their own decisions about spiritual beliefs. It credits each individual with possessing the capacity to make rational decisions and frees hearts and minds from the corrosive impact of ingrained prejudices. The Bible confirms the result of such an investigation of reality:

> And ye shall know the truth, and the truth shall make you free.[21]

---

20 Abdu'l-Bahá, *The Promulgation of World Peace*, p. 433.
21 *Bible*, John 8:32, King James Version.

The Nature of Reality

Reality contains within it boundless details, each of which pertains to a particular aspect of life. None of us can hope to explore everything there is to know. Fortunately, in the Writings of the world's most recent wisdom tradition, we have been given a summary of the most important features of reality that a wise person will assuredly discover.

> Reality is one; and when found, it will unify all mankind. Reality is the love of God. Reality is the knowledge of God. Reality is justice. Reality is the oneness or solidarity of mankind. Reality is international peace. Reality is the knowledge of verities. Reality unifies humanity.[22]

This is a definition of a reality that remains to be widely discovered. It may seem at first dissonant with our experience of the world but only because this potential Reality has not yet been fully realized. When we are called upon to individually investigate reality, we must study not just reality as it currently exists but also the inevitable reality that approaches. We know the world is changing.

The hopeful message above suggests a brighter future ahead, though certainly not without serious struggles to obtain it. The opening phrase "Reality is one" emphasizes that unity—the oneness of God and religion and humanity—is the gravity that binds everything together from the bright centers of the universe to the planets farthest from them, from the extremes of diversity to the consciousness that:

> Ye are the fruits of one tree, and the leaves of one branch. We cherish the hope that the light of justice may shine upon the world and sanctify it from tyranny.[23]

---

22 'Abdu'l-Bahá, *The Promulgation of Universal Peace*
23 Bahá'u'lláh, *Fountain of Wisdom*

The Foundation of All Virtues

Virtues are moral attitudes or character traits necessary for us to achieve a true understanding of reality and respond to it appropriately. We can only experience virtues when we live within a social community. People living by themselves cannot lie to others, cannot steal from others. Only in a social setting do virtues become a reality and take on meaning. Of all the virtues that can be acquired by an individual, one can be considered foundational.

> Truthfulness is the foundation of all human virtues. Without truthfulness progress and success, in all the worlds of God, are impossible for any soul. When this holy attribute is established in man, all the divine qualities will also be acquired.[24]

Truthfulness contributes to everything we do, consequently untruthfulness impedes the progress of everything and is a chief instrument of the destructive process of disintegration. The lack of truthfulness and the crisis of trust it engenders is at the heart of business and governmental corruption, infidelity, personal disrespect, political unrest and break-ups in relationships. Truthfulness is a solution to deceit, dishonesty, hypocrisy, fraud, misinformation, unreliability, treachery, deception, insincerity and indirection. It is difficult to imagine a future world that does not embrace truthfulness as a primary condition for the success of society because untruthfulness is the direct cause of so many of our problems.

For an independent investigation of reality to be meaningful requires total truthfulness with ourselves as well. We must ask ourselves if we can honestly set aside our previous conceptions of reality, our prejudices and comforting rituals, the many white lies we have been telling ourselves, the coercion of friends and family and clergy, and then honestly and objectively evaluate what we learn.

---

24 'Abdu'l-Bahá, quoted in Shoghi Effendi, *The Advent of Divine Justice*.

This can be hard work. But it is part of the constructive process, and when we engage in it we are working to defeat the forces of the destructive process that rely on ignorance and untruthfulness for success. This is the value of independent, rational thinking versus blind faith in the conclusions of others.

Chapter 3:
The Oneness of a Diverse Humanity

In this book, we will write a lot about the rational need for the unification of humanity and society, but what do we mean by those terms? Generally, when we speak of humanity, we are referring to a collection of human beings, and when we speak of society, we are referring to the organized structure that humans have created to organize and govern themselves. As we investigate reality for ourselves—"reality" meaning the physical, emotional and spiritual nature of the human condition—basic questions emerge.

What Are Humans?

Are humans essentially highly evolved animals? The theory of evolution proposes that changes in species can occur over time through the agency of natural selection. This suggests that humans, who share 99 percent of their DNA with apes, are animals. The taxonomic classification system uses a hierarchical model to organize living organisms into increasingly specific categories, placing humans in the Animalia kingdom within the same order as primates, also suggesting that humans are considered by scientists to be animals.

While this similarity makes sense anatomically, which is the organizational schema for classification, it seems clear that the taxonomy does not include other important distinguishing information—spirituality and intellectual capacity, for example—because the classification was limited to physical similarities.

It seems obvious, however, that humans are much more than just smarter animals. Certainly, humans are capable of elevated levels of rational and critical thinking. It is hard to imagine apes or dolphins thinking about the spiritual nature of their species. Humans have also developed language, which allows them to share knowledge and communicate both tangible and abstract concepts. Rationally, one can argue that humans stand alone in a category above the animal realm, as discussed in *The Soul of Humanity*. The lower realms of existence, then—the mineral, vegetable and animal realms—each acquire the virtues of the lower realms but cannot achieve those of a higher realm without intervention. According to this logic, humans reside above the animal realm and below the realm of the Divine.

> If it be claimed that the intellectual reality of man belongs to the world of nature—that it is a part of the whole—we ask is it possible for the part to contain virtues which the whole does not possess? For instance, is it possible for the drop to contain virtues of which the aggregate body of the sea is deprived? Is it possible for a leaf to be imbued with virtues which are lacking in the whole tree? Is it possible that the extraordinary faculty of reason in man is animal in character and quality?

> On the other hand... in man there is present this supernatural force or faculty which discovers the realities of things and which possesses the power of idealization or intellection. It is capable of discovering scientific laws, and science we know is not a tangible reality. The mind itself, reason itself, is an ideal reality and not tangible....

> [The] human reality stands between the higher and the lower in man, between the world of the animal and the

> world of Divinity. When the animal proclivity in man becomes predominant, he sinks even lower than the brute. When the heavenly powers are triumphant in his nature, he becomes the noblest and most superior being in the world of creation. All the imperfections found in the animal are found in man. In him there is antagonism, hatred and selfish struggle for existence; in his nature lurk jealousy, revenge, ferocity, cunning, hypocrisy, greed, injustice and tyranny. So to speak, the reality of man is clad in the outer garment of the animal, the habiliments of the world of nature, the world of darkness, imperfections and unlimited baseness.[25]

The most recent wisdom tradition confirms that only humans are capable making ethical decisions and have been imbued with a "rational soul." To some, elevating humans to a status above that of animals seems like arrogance, but while the existence of a rational soul cannot yet be scientifically proven, it also cannot be scientifically refuted.

Is it possible that Teilhard du Chardin was right? He wrote, "We are not human beings having a spiritual experience. We are spiritual beings having a human [physical] experience." Perhaps we should take this concept one step further, because…

> …the rational soul does not merely occupy a private sphere, but is an active participant in a social order.[26]

The Oneness of Humanity

Previously, we discussed the concept of the oneness of humankind, which arises from the concepts of the oneness of God and the oneness of religions in their foundational spiritual principles.

---

25 'Abdu'l-Bahá, *The Promulgation of Universal Peace*, p. 465
26 The Universal House of Justice, *One Common Faith*,

> All men are of one family; the crown of humanity rests on the head of every human being. In the eyes of the Creator all His children are equal... He does not favor this nation nor that nation, all alike are His creatures. This being so, why should we make divisions, separating one race from another? Why should we create barriers of superstition and tradition bringing discord and hatred among the people?[27]

This does not mean that all humans are equivalent in intelligence, strength and athletic ability; it does not mean that men can bear children as women do; it does mean that everyone has the same artistic gifts, religious beliefs or eye color, hair color, skin color.

> The only difference between members of the human family is that of degree. Some are like children who are ignorant and must be educated until they arrive at maturity. Some are like the sick and must be treated with tenderness and care. None are bad or evil! We must not be repelled by these poor children. We must treat them with great kindness, teaching the ignorant and tenderly nursing the sick.[28]

In earlier pages, we considered the numerous troubles that confront the world today, but consider the chief cause of these problems.

> Are not these intermittent crises that convulse present-day society due primarily to the lamentable inability of the world's recognized leaders to read aright the signs of the times, to rid themselves once for all of their preconceived ideas and fettering creeds, and to reshape the machinery of their respective governments

---

27 'Abdu'l-Bahá, *Paris Talks*
28 'Abdu'l-Bahá, *Paris Talks*

> according to those standards that are implicit in [the truth] of the Oneness of Mankind…?²⁹

Clearly, history teaches that it is imaginary or insignificant differences between the peoples of the earth and their claimed habitats and diverse cultures that keep the black heart of disunity beating.

> God created one earth and one mankind to people it. Man has no other habitation, but man himself has come forth and proclaimed imaginary boundary lines and territorial restrictions, naming them Germany, France, Russia, etc. And torrents of precious blood are spilled in defense of these imaginary divisions of our one human habitation, under the delusion of a fancied and limited patriotism.³⁰

The Concept of "Race" Is a Lie

The subheading above is a direct quote from *Scientific American*, May 14, 2019. The American Society of Human Genetics, the largest professional organization of scientists in the field, explained in an essay, "The science of genetics demonstrates that humans cannot be divided into biologically distinct subcategories…" and it "challenges the traditional concept of different races of humans as biologically separate and distinct. This is validated by many decades of research." In other words, "race itself is a social construct" with no biological basis.³¹

More than 130 leading population geneticists condemned the idea that genetic differences account for the economic, political, social and behavioral diversity around the world.³² A 2018 article

---

29 Shoghi Effendi, *Call to the Nations*
30 'Abdu'l-Bahá, *The Promulgation of Universal Peace*
31 https://www.cell.com/ajhg/fulltext/S0002-9297(18)30363-X.
32 https://bit.ly/3P3Pbf3. Link is to an article entitled "Geneticists say popular book misrepresents research on human revolution" at blogs.nature.com.

in Scientific American stated that "there is a broad scientific consensus that when it comes to genes there is just as much diversity within racial and ethnic groups as there is across them."[33] And the Human Genome Project has confirmed that the genomes found around the globe are 99.9 percent identical in every person.[34] Clearly, the very idea of different "races" is nonsense… and comparatively new.

If you Google "how many races are there," you will get answers ranging from three to seven or more. These are definitions created for specific purposes, such as census counting, and have nothing to do with the scientific concept of race.

Research by statistician Joseph Chang at Yale discovered that the most recent common ancestor of everyone alive today lived just 3,600 years ago. "Our findings suggest a remarkable proposition," he concluded. "No matter the languages we speak or the color of our skin, we share ancestors who planted rice on the banks of the Yangtze, who first domesticated horses on the steppes of the Ukraine, who hunted giant sloths in the forests of North and South America, and who labored to build the Great Pyramid of Khufu."[35]

Scientifically, then, it is our experiences and our culture, not our DNA, that account for most of our differences. While ethnicity is real, there are only minor differences between ethnic groups. There is no such thing as "race"—only racism.[36] And the consequences of racism are horrible.

---

33 https://bit.ly/3EmOpVi. This link is to an article entitled "Effort to Diversify Research Raises Thorny Questions of Race" in the online version of *Scientific American*.

34 https://bit.ly/45OgbX7. This link is to an opinion piece entitled "Why your DNA test won't reveal the real you" in the online version of *The Globe and Mail*.

35 Quoted in the book by Adam Rutherford, *A Brief History of Everyone Who Ever Lived: The Human Story Retold Through Our Genes*, The Experiment; Reprint edition (September 4, 2018).

36 https://blogs.scientificamerican.com/observations/the-concept-of-race-is-a-lie/.

Since each individual on the planet is unique in DNA and experiences, how can we possibly divide people into "races?" Where do we draw the lines? Does it not seem more productive to simply appreciate each individual as distinctly different but collectively unified in their humanity?

Unity in Diversity

The diversity of humanity is both physical and mental. Every individual is distinct from every other individual physically, but each also has a different perspective on the world. Each of these unique perspectives is a window opening up knowledge to humanity. Diversity is built into creation and the distinctive thoughts and ideas of every person contribute to innovation and discovery. Collectively, however, all these diverse people who are having these unique thoughts can become unified to achieve a universal goal.

Our most recent wisdom tradition has compared the world to the human body for a lesson about unity in diversity. There is, indeed, no other physical existence to which we can reasonably look for such a rich metaphor.

> Human society is composed not of a mass of merely differentiated cells but of associations of individuals, each one of whom is endowed with intelligence and will; nevertheless, the modes of operation that characterize man's biological nature illustrate fundamental principles of existence. Chief among these is that of unity in diversity.

> Paradoxically, it is precisely the wholeness and complexity of the order constituting the human body—and the perfect integration into it of the body's cells—that permit the full realization of the distinctive capacities inherent in each of these component elements. No cell

> lives apart from the body, whether in contributing to its functioning or in deriving its share from the well-being of the whole. The physical well-being thus achieved finds its purpose in making possible the expression of human consciousness; that is to say, the purpose of biological development transcends the mere existence of the body and its parts.

> What is true of the life of the individual has its parallels in human society. The human species is an organic whole, the leading edge of the evolutionary process. That human consciousness necessarily operates through an infinite diversity of individual minds and motivations detracts in no way from its essential unity.[37]

Unity vs. Uniformity

The oneness of humankind in no way suggests that humans must conform to some definition of uniformity. The principle of unity in diversity creates guardrails to prevent authoritarian enforcement of unnecessary conformity. It preserves and in fact promotes inherited cultural identities and diverse ethnic backgrounds. It reconciles nationalism with internationalism and racialism with universalism. Cultural, ethnic and national differences that are not fundamental and contrary to the spirit of unity are seen for what they truly are—individual and creative expressions of a people unified through their humanity. Tolerance for minor differences is replaced by appreciation for the richness of these expressions. The point of this concept is neither to minimize differences nor make a false dichotomy of unity and diversity, but to bring to human interactions a spirit of love and freedom from uniformity.

---

37 The Universal House of Justice, *The Prosperity of Humankind*, p. 1

> The diversity in the human family should be the cause of love and harmony, as it is in music where many different notes blend together in the making of a perfect chord. If you meet those of a different race and colour from yourself, do not mistrust them and withdraw yourself into your shell of conventionality, but rather be glad and show them kindness.[38]

Logically, unity in diversity contributes to the constructive process of integration we discussed earlier. But what if there exists diversity without unity? In many places today, this is the default condition. Unfortunately, when diversity is not accompanied by a spirit of unity, it contributes to the destructive process of disintegration. Put simply, whatever contributes to disunity is destructive long-term, and whatever contributes to greater unity is constructive, leading us closer to a more mature society. Rationally, diversity should be a chief cause of unity, but unsurprisingly, for thousands of years, we seem to have gotten it backwards.

As you may expect, it is one thing to adopt a conceptual framework such as the oneness of humanity and an appreciation for diversity. But it is quite another thing to put it into practice despite the durability of old paradigms and past grudges. Because we have a great distance to go toward the goal, this principle can be considered a beacon of truth that illuminates the path to maturity.

The Cohesion of Society Is at Risk

Since early in the twenty-first century, the term "identity crisis"—so often used to describe an individual who lacks a confirmed sense of how he compares and differentiates from everyone else or how she fits into society—has been a defining feature of our current times. The forces of our global age are blurring the boundaries that give

---

[38] 'Abdu'l-Bahá, quoted in Shoghi Effendi, *The Advent of Divine Justice*, p. 32

people and groups their identities and removing or thwarting the secure sense of belonging that traditionally has been enjoyed by group members. The result is often a state of confusion, insecurity, conflict, and ever-bolder assertions of differences. Oddly, as a deeply felt sense of human oneness has been developing among more people, the opposing categories of identity have multiplied. According to our most recent wisdom tradition:

> Humanity is gripped by a crisis of identity, as various peoples and groups struggle to define themselves, their place in the world, and how they should act. Without a vision of shared identity and common purpose, they fall into competing ideologies and power struggles. Seemingly countless permutations of "us" and "them" define group identities ever more narrowly and in contrast to one another. Over time, this splintering into divergent interest groups has weakened the cohesion of society itself.[39]

As social psychologists explain, social identity is self-defined in ways that have significant emotional meaning for the individual. It typically entails deep ties of empathy, solidarity, belonging and love. These deep ties differ from the more cerebral or emotionally shallow bonds of universal human connection that may arise, for example, from a rational commitment to the equal moral worth of all persons.[40] Social identity, then, is a powerful force.

To confront humanity's crisis of identity, some thinkers have proposed a newly enlightened and inclusive form of nationalism as a

---

[39] Universal House of Justice, letter to the Bahá'ís of the World, 18 January 2019. "On humanity's crisis of identity and the principle of human oneness, "see also: Universal House of Justice, letter to the Followers of Bahá'u'lláh in the Democratic Republic of the Congo, 1 November 2022.

[40] Monroe, K. R., Hankin, J., & Van Vechten, R.B. (2000). "The psychological foundations of identity politics." *The Annual Review of Political Science*, 3(1), 419-447. 2000.

big tent social category within which various narrower identities and affiliations can be contained and reconciled.[41] Historically, however, solutions grounded in national identity or other similar concepts have struggled to resolve the identity crisis.

As a counterpoint to these suggestions, the latest wisdom tradition proposes that only a collective identity[42] rooted in a recognition of human oneness can relieve the tensions that surround our current identity crisis.

> Rival conceptions about the primacy of a particular people are peddled to the exclusion of the truth that humanity is on a common journey in which all are protagonists. Consider how radically different such a fragmented conception of human identity is from the one that follows from a recognition of the oneness of humanity. In this perspective, the diversity that characterizes the human family, far from contradicting its oneness, endows it with richness. Unity… contains the essential concept of diversity, distinguishing it from uniformity. It is through love for all people, and by subordinating lesser loyalties to the best interests of humankind, that the unity of the world can be realized and the infinite expressions of human diversity find their highest fulfilment.[43]

---

41 For example, see: Amy Chua, *Political Tribes: Group Instincts and the Fate of Nations* (New York: Penguin Press, 2018); Francis Fukuyama, *Identity: The Demand for Dignity and the Politics of Resentment* (New York: Farrar, Straus and Giroux, 2018); Mark Lilla, *The Once and Future Liberal* (New York: Harper, 2017); Yascha Mounk, *The Great Experiment: Why Diverse Democracies Fall Apart and What We Can Do About It* (New York: Penguin Press, 2022).

42 For the purposes of this chapter, the terms, "group identity," "collective identity," "social identity" and "identity" are used interchangeably.

43 Universal House of Justice, letter to the Bahá'ís of the World, 18 January 2019. Added. See change.

In contemporary discourse, this is a radical departure from the way that our shared humanity is generally understood and discussed. Many other existing concepts for resolving the identity crisis are widely recognized as homogenizing but are dismissed as being too remote from everyday life to have sufficient relevance to society in general.

The concept offered by the latest wisdom tradition, however, offers a different vision. Far from threatening or contradicting the obvious diversity of humankind, it suggests that a universal human identity is uniquely equipped to ensure the security and flourishing of identities specific to individuals and their various affiliations and communities.

Two Underlying Tensions

Underlying humanity's crisis of identity, two "long-standing tensions, or apparent contradictions… complicate its resolution. The first tension pertains directly to the nature of traditional group identities themselves."[44] On one hand, traditional "bounded" identities—those that are constrained by including some kinds of people but not others—are fundamentally susceptible to instability, conflict and destructiveness, over time revealing an ugly face.

On the other hand, at the group level, greater diversity of all forms is vital to a group's strength and stability. Diversity provides a broader basis for community, collective action and mutual support. For individual members of a group, greater diversity provides less group differentiation but more advancement of each member's self-concept of being humans who yearn for recognition, inclusion and expression.

Almost all groups exist somewhere along an exclusive-to-inclusive spectrum, which means they possess a dual nature resulting

---

44 Sabet, Shahrzad, "The Crisis of Identity," published in The Bahá'í World, January 17, 2023; Available at: https://bahaiworld.bahai.org/library/the-crisis-of-identity/.

in built-in tensions between the two extreme positions. This duality is defined more explicitly by our most recent wisdom tradition, which explains that the differences between these extremes...

> ... are of two kinds. One is the cause of annihilation and is like the antipathy existing among warring nations and conflicting tribes who seek each other's destruction, uprooting one another's families, depriving one another of rest and comfort and unleashing carnage. The other kind which is a token of diversity is the essence of perfection and the cause of the appearance of the bestowals of the Most Glorious Lord.[45]

The two extremes of this spectrum, which are constantly pulling in different directions, leave traditional bounded identities in a state of chronic tension and instability with no resolution. Consequently, social identities are continuously vulnerable to conflict and destructive behavior.

Even worse, this tension within bounded groups can be ramped up when they encounter forces and movements that are unbounded or more diverse. Examples of such forces are economic globalization, enhanced transborder communication, greater universality of moral institutions, expanding consciousness of humanity's oneness, and the countless interdependencies that produced a catastrophic climate crisis and propagated a deadly virus around the globe. Our increasingly global age, with all its porousness and fluidity, is challenging humanity's earnest yearning for rootedness and belonging.

A great irony lies hidden within the rapid evolution of this age. As our shared consciousness of the physical, social, moral, and economic space we inhabit is expanded to include the population of the entire planet, uncertainty about its many bounded groupings intensifies to produce a broader tension between the emotional tug

---

45 'Abdu'l-Bahá, *Selections from the Writings of 'Abdu'l-Bahá*. Available at www.bahai.org/r/583780535

of bounded identities and affiliations on one hand and the intense pull of universalist forces and aspirations on the other.

So, can humanity's fundamental oneness be reconciled with its obvious diversity to at last achieve peace and tranquility? According to our newest wisdom tradition, it is through the recognition of the oneness of humanity that the diversity of humankind thrives and finds its highest fulfillment. In a practical sense, then, what would be the features of an identity rooted in the oneness of humanity?

An Identity Rooted in Humankind's Oneness

The authors believe that an identity based on the principle of the oneness of humanity is qualitatively unique compared to all other social identities because of two distinguishing features. These features enable such an identity to stabilize and empower individual identities in ways that other broader affiliations such as nationality cannot.

Of course, identities and specific aspects of them that cannot be reconciled with the principle of human oneness—those rooted in racial superiority or some other form of enmity toward others—should *not* be preserved or empowered. Over time, they must be abandoned.

Non-exclusionary

The first distinctive feature of an identity rooted in humanity's essential oneness is its *non-exclusionary* nature. This kind of identity is completely unbound and has no concept of otherness. This feature alone makes such an identity stand in contrast to all other traditional social identities that have defined outsiders and so are manifestly bounded and exclusionary. A non-exclusionary identity will ultimately lead to a deeper appreciation of our broader interdependence with our entire environment including non-human life.

Non-contingency

The second unique feature is *non-contingency*. Scientific studies widely confirm that virtually all other group identities are socially constructed.⁴⁶ They are real, of course, in their material consequences, or in our experience and valuation of them. But the commonalities on which these identities are based are contingent—dependent—on a wide spectrum of social constructs and transitory phenomena such as evolving beliefs about social and biological reality, contested details of history, social or demographic parameters for membership, even shared experiences of injustice.⁴⁷

The world's most recent wisdom tradition elaborated on the impermanence and inherent contingency of the many identities that traditionally bind humans together:

> In the contingent world there are many collective centers which are conducive to association and unity between the children of men. For example, patriotism is a collective center; nationalism is a collective center; identity of interests is a collective center; political alliance is a collective center; the union of ideals is a collective center, and the prosperity of the world of humanity is dependent upon the organization and promotion of the collective centers. Nevertheless, all the above institutions are, in reality, the matter and not the substance, accidental and not eternal—temporary and not everlasting. With the appearance of great revolutions and upheavals, all these collective centers are swept away.⁴⁸

---

46 W.C. Byrd, et al, "Biological determinism and racial essentialism: The ideological double helix of racial inequality," The ANNALS of the American Academy of Political and Social Science 661, no. 1.

47 One might object that an identity based on gender is an exception to this observation. But a large part of what constitutes gender—our ideas about what different genders are and how members of each should behave and feel—is socially constructed. The Universal House of Justice wrote in a letter to the Bahá'ís of Iran dated 2 March 2013: "The rational soul has no gender or race, ethnicity or class…"

48 'Abdu'l-Bahá, "Tablets of the Divine Place," 14: Tablet to the Bahá'ís of the United States and Canada.

When taken together, these two features of an identity rooted in the humanity's essential oneness—that it is non-exclusionary and non-contingent—carry far-reaching implications.

Establishing Fundamental Security

The two features of a collective identity rooted in the oneness of humanity—a universal human identity—provide the essential and immovable conditions of inclusion to produce an identity that is thoroughly stable and safe.

By contrast, traditional bounded identities (there are outsiders) and contingently grounded identities (socially constructed and subject to reconstruction) have parameters for membership that can be contested or redefined to either banish or welcome newly defined castes. They are inherently unstable. The threat of excluding some persons can come from outside the group (social pressure, non-members) or from within the group ("othering" of some persons or affiliations.) The question of "who belongs?" can never be fully closed. Today's insiders can be tomorrow's outsiders.

The topic of nationalism highlights the dilemma. The narrative of a national identity is perpetually recontested and retold. The parameters of otherness are regularly gerrymandered. Even in long-consolidated nations and democracies, the following unsettled question often arises: "Who counts as a 'real' national and who doesn't?"

The authors believe that only a collective identity that is unbounded and non-contingently grounded—one rooted in the fundamental truth of the oneness of humanity—can deliver the conditions for the fundamental security of all people. Everyone belongs simply because everyone is human. Full stop.

Empirical Research

Many people believe that science has no place in matters of faith and religion, but that is not true. It is possible to scientifically investigate whether recognition of the oneness of humanity can have an impact on individuals. Empirical research in psychology has confirmed that it does by providing a sense of greater security.

A substantial body of research analyzed by Shahrzad Sabet, co-director of the Center on Modernity in Transition (COMIT), has found that a condition identified as "felt security" relieved intergroup hostility and yielded a posture of empathy, care, and openness to "out-groups"[49] comprised of excluded individuals. The opposite condition of "felt threat" increased hostility and conflict within one's own group. Clearly, a sense of security is conducive to more caring and empathetic relations with those who hold different bounded identities.[50]

---

49 O. Gillath, et al, "Attachment, caregiving, and volunteering: Placing volunteerism in an attachment theoretical framework," Personal Relationships 12, no. 4 (2005): 425-446; M. Mikulincer, et al, "Attachment theory and reactions to others' needs: Evidence that activation of the sense of attachment security promotes empathic responses," Journal of Personality and Social Psychology 81, no. 1 (2001): 1205-24; M. Mikulincer, et al, "Attachment theory and concern for others' welfare: evidence that activation of the sense of secure base promotes endorsement of self-transcendence values," Basic and Applied Social Psychology 25, no. 4 (2003): 299-312; M. Mikulincer, et al, "Attachment, caregiving, and altruism: Boosting attachment security increases compassion and helping," Journal of Personality and Social Psychology 89, no. 5 (2005): 817-839.

50 M. B. Brewer, "The importance of being we: Human nature and intergroup relations," American Psychologist 62, no. 8 (2007): 728-738; M. B. Brewer, et al, "An evolutionary perspective on social identity: Revisiting groups," in Evolution and social psychology, eds. M. Schaller, et al, (Madison, CT: Psychology Press, 2006), 143-161; L. Huddy, "From group identity to political cohesion and commitment," in The Oxford Handbook of Political Psychology, eds. L. Huddy, et al, (New York: Oxford University Press, 2013), 737-773; D. R. Kinder, "Prejudice and politics," in The Oxford Handbook of Political Psychology, eds. L. Huddy, et al, (New York: Oxford University Press, 2013), 812-851. See also: L. S. Richman, et al, "Reactions to discrimination, stigmatization, ostracism, and other forms of interpersonal rejection: A multimotive model," Psychological Review 116, no. 2 (2009): 365-383; J. M. Twenge, et al, "Social exclusion decreases prosocial behavior," Journal of Personality and Social Psychology 92, no. 1 (2007): 56-66; W.A.Warburton, et al, "When ostracism leads to aggression: The moderating effects of control deprivation," Journal

A second group of studies further suggests that identifying with the humanity of others is associated with a considerably higher level of "felt security." After analyzing in-depth interviews with Nazi supporters, bystanders, and rescuers of Jews, political psychologist Kristen Monroe determined that those who saw themselves foremost as part of all humankind experienced much higher levels of felt security.[51] In a different study, brain imaging in neuropsychology revealed that the amygdala—that part of the brain involved in the experience of fear and aggression—became highly active when a subject was shown faces from different races. But when subjects were first primed to think of people as individual human beings rather than members of groups, the amygdala did not react.[52]

Such empirical research suggests that identifying with the oneness of humankind is associated with a greater sense of security, which relieves intergroup hostility and establishes greater empathy, care, altruism and openness toward those previously thought of as others. "A framework of deep, all-pervasive security delivers not merely a stable equilibrium of peaceful coexistence, but rather, optimal conditions for the vibrancy and flourishing of particular identities, and of human diversity more broadly," political scientist Shahrzad Sabet wrote, adding that the most recent wisdom tradition "directly and explicitly ties the non-contingency of universal love to a spiritual source."[53]

---

of Experimental Social Psychology 42, no. 2 (2006): 213-220.

51 K. R. Monroe, Heart of altruism: Perception of a common humanity, (Princeton: Princeton University Press, 1996). K. R. Monroe, The hand of compassion: portraits of moral choice during the holocaust, (Princeton: Princeton University Press, 2006).

52 M.E. Wheeler, S. T. Fiske, et al, "Controlling racial prejudice: social-cognitive goals affect amygdala and stereotype activation," Psychol Sci. 16, no. 1 (2005): 56-63.

53 Sabet, Shahrzad, "The Crisis of Identity," published in The Bahá'í World, January 17, 2023; Available at: https://bahaiworld.bahai.org/library/the-crisis-of-identity/.

> "... fraternity, love and kindness based upon family, nativity, race or an attitude of altruism are neither sufficient nor permanent since all of them are limited, restricted and liable to change and disruption. For in the family there is discord and alienation; among sons of the same fatherland strife and internecine warfare are witnessed; between those of a given race, hostility and hatred are frequent; and even among the altruists varying aspects of opinion and lack of unselfish devotion give little promise of permanent and indestructible unity among mankind ... the foundation of real brotherhood, the cause of loving co-operation and reciprocity and the source of real kindness and unselfish devotion is none other than the breaths of the Holy Spirit. Without this influence and animus it is impossible. We may be able to realize some degrees of fraternity through other motives but these are limited associations and subject to change. When human brotherhood is founded upon the Holy Spirit, it is eternal, changeless, unlimited."[54]

The fundamental spiritual principle underlying universal peace and prosperity is the oneness of humanity.

---

54 Abdu'l-Bahá, *The Promulgation of Universal Peace*, pp. 385-386.

Chapter 4:
Sin and Morality

Any discussion of humanity must include the topic of sin. What is sin? Is it the default nature of a human being to be sinful? Can the sins of ancestors be inherited, condemning us to judgement for sinful acts we did not personally commit? The ancient concept of sin lies at the core of all the world's wisdom traditions. But as usual, religious authorities charged with interpreting the Teachings and drumming their manmade notions of sin into the minds of their followers have created a tangled mess of meaning from which guilt—the main cudgel used by all who wish to assert their control—nevertheless manifests in all its influential power.

What is Sin?

Sin is a religious concept regarded as the deliberate and purposeful violation of the will of God—an immoral act considered to be a transgression of Divine law. In this sense, sin is always personal and has nothing to do with the community. Religions offer an array of sometimes vague offenses that qualify as sinful. Some teach that there are various categories of sin (original sin, venial sin, mortal sin, unforgivable sin) and offer a rich vocabulary of synonyms (iniquity, transgression, wickedness, mischief, et cetera.) The Old Testament gives us a list of sins that God Himself purportedly instructed humankind to avoid. These are popularly called the Ten Commandments. Pope Gregory I in 600 AD compiled a list of seven "deadly" sins—lust, gluttony, greed, laziness, wrath, envy and pride—accompanied by a second list of virtues he thought should be highlighted.

Sin generally does not refer to acts that are merely unlawful under civil law, but like common crimes, sin is said to require suitable punishments usually specified in the scriptures or traditions of one's religion. As expected, the recommended punishments swiftly administered by society vary greatly and range from shunning and banishment to mutilation and death by stoning. In Christianity, however, the spiritual penalty for sinful behavior—spiritual death, meaning separation from God—is likewise harsh though delayed.

> **For the wages of sin is death…**[55]

> **They will suffer the punishment of eternal destruction, away from the presence of the Lord and from the glory of his might.**[56]

> **For if we go on sinning deliberately after receiving the knowledge of the truth, there no longer remains a sacrifice for sins, but only a fearful expectation of judgment and of raging fire that will consume the enemies of God.**[57]

Where does sin come from? Our most recent wisdom tradition explains it this way:

---

55 *The Bible*, Romans 6:23.
56 *The Bible*, 2 Thessalonians 1:9 (ESV)
57 *The Bible*, Hebrews 10:26

> All sin is prompted by the dictates of nature. These dictates of nature, which are among the hallmarks of corporeal existence, are not sins with respect to the animal but are sins with regard to man. The animal is the source of imperfections such as anger, lust, envy, greed, cruelty, and pride. All these blameworthy qualities are found in the nature of the animal, and do not constitute sins with regard to the animal, whereas they are sins with regard to man.[58]

Guilt—the emotional discomfort resulting from recognizing one's sins—coupled with the threat of damnation and torment as consequences, has often been used by religious leaders to manipulate behavior. But guilt only works if those who need to be controlled believe their offenses deserve retribution and that the authorities—typically religious leaders and their God—will carry out the punishments. Ironically, countless sinful acts of unjustified barbarism and murder in the name of God's intolerance of sin have been committed over the centuries along with a sea of psychological trauma, broken families, and the confiscation of wealth, which is too often a primary goal. Rationally, then, it seems that the ferocious efforts to beat the sin out of the sinful often results in even greater sins by the so-called authorities, the same priests who are often first to defy the dawn of a new wisdom tradition.

It is clear, then, that sin often involves at least two sinners—first, the person committing a specific sin, and second, the person who judges the sinner. Since religious texts all state or infer that no one is without sin, the individuals who criticize or judge sinners are likewise sinners, thus they are in no position to judge. If the person judging another's sinful behavior expects a sinless life from the one being judged, then sinlessness should be expected from the judge as well. This makes no sense because it is impossible.

---

58 'Abdu'l-Bahá, *Some Answered Questions*.

When a crowd of critics were about to stone a woman caught in the act of adultery, Jesus admonished them with these words:

> **He that is without sin among you, let him first cast a stone at her.**[59]

An additional problem arises when someone claims authority to judge another's sins, or when society gives someone authority to judge sinful behavior. The act of judgement itself creates a division within the community, which works against unity, and those granted such power can ultimately become known as representatives of God on Earth who are entitled to issue judgments with absolute power.

The Problem of "Original Sin"

Outdated concepts of the essential sinful nature of man go back to a concept of "original sin" that originated among early Christian thinkers. Do humans inherit the sins of their ancestors? According to the Roman Catholic Church and some Protestant denominations, humans carry through natural generation the debt—meaning the guilt and the consequences—of the original sin of Adam and Eve. Never mind that these two famous personages are mythical, so they never could have sinned, but if they were historical figures, this concept means that all humans are born with a sinful nature and, in a sense, have already sinned as infants due to their inheritance. They are already burdened with debt. Only through baptism and the grace of God can they be saved from eternal damnation.

Other Christian traditions, such as the Eastern Orthodox Church, split hairs by believing that humans do not inherit the guilt of original sin but only the judgment or effects of it. All humans, then, are accused of having a corrupt nature making them prone to sin but are not actually guilty of sinning. Even so, humans still require baptism and God's grace for salvation.

---

59   *The Bible*, John 8:7

Original sin is not an explicit teaching in the Old Testament or the recorded words of Jesus, weakening the authority of this teaching. Adherents to this belief hold to questionable interpretations of a passage in Romans 5:12-21 and a few other texts of Paul to substantiate the concept.

Original sin, however, seems to contradict the doctrine of free will and moral responsibility. It is certainly incompatible with the justice and goodness of God because it means innocent children must be punished for their ancestors' wrongdoings. In a way, it appears to blame God for creating defective humans who are born with sin. Perhaps most troubling is that it exaggerates the effects of someone else's sin on an individual and minimizes the role of personal sin in causing misery and alienation from God.

Is Sinfulness the Default State of Humankind?

There is no question that humankind is imperfect. We all make mistakes and occasionally commit sins. But if we were to believe the teachings of many religious leaders today, we might conclude that humans are basically sinful or evil by nature. This dark and pessimistic view of God's creation does not inspire confidence in humankind's ability to build an ever-advancing civilization. It does, however, develop a strong, emotional need for a solution—perhaps a Savior who can expunge our record, even if temporarily, by removing our sins. During previous eras, when societies were less educated and required a simpler message to instill discipline, this simplified, fear-based message emphasizing our persistent shortcomings and the likely consequences for misdeeds may have been necessary.

An opposing view from the latest wisdom tradition, however, is now available to us and is a more rational and positive explanation of humankind's true nature. Instead of being naturally drawn to evil, humankind is basically good. Because humans dwell in a realm of existence between animals and the Divine, humans have a dual nature—a baser, animal nature and the capacity to acquire Divine attributes or virtues.

> Evil is imperfection. Sin is the state of man in the world of the baser nature, for in nature exist defects such as injustice, tyranny, hatred, hostility, strife: these are characteristics of the lower plane of nature. These are the sins of the world... Through education we must free ourselves from these imperfections. The Prophets of God have been sent, the Holy Books have been written, so that man may be made free.[60]

In our opinion, the freedom mentioned above suggests freedom from the gravity of our lower nature so we can rise through an independent search for reality toward our largely untapped human capacities to love, cooperate, contribute and even make sacrifices for those we love—hopefully an ever-growing circle of people that eventually can encompass everyone through our love for all humankind.

> If evil has a name, it is surely the deliberate violation of the hard-won covenants of peace and reconciliation by which people of goodwill seek to escape the past and to build together a new future.[61]

What is Satan?

A popular notion today is that evil, except for original sin, originates from an Evil One sometimes called the Devil or Satan with a legion of demons that tempt or trick us into sinning—and often succeeds. A deeper look into the original concepts of this Evil One go back thousands of years with roots in various religious and cultural

---

60 'Abdu'l-Bahá, *Paris Talks*, p. 177.
61 The Universal House of Justice, *One Common Faith*.

traditions. Many experts say the name Satan is not a proper name but derives from the Hebrew word "ha-Satan," which translates as "the opposer" or "the adversary," more a simple description of the character's function in folkloric tales as the opponent of God's creation. A common alternative term for this anti-hero is the Devil, which comes from the Greek word "diabolos" meaning "accuser" or "slanderer," also descriptions of the Devil's multiple roles.

Over time, due to folkloric drift, Satan's identity and provenance evolved to suit different cultures, storylines and purposes. During the height of the Persian Archaemenid Empire c. 550 BCE, the influential figure of Satan was adopted by the Jews but not considered a totally evil being in the Jewish Bible. The word "satan" first appears in the Old Testament as a supernatural figure in the Book of Numbers using the word "satan" to indicate an adversary:

> Balaam's departure aroused the wrath of Elohim, and the Angel of Yahweh stood in the road as a satan against him.[62]

In 2 Samuel 24, God sends this same Angel of Yahweh to inflict a three-day plague against Israel as punishment for David who took a census without His approval. The plague killed 70,000 people, an act of indescribable malevolence against innocents that is easier to pin on the Angel rather than God. This same story is repeated in 1 Chronicles 21:1 but replaces the Angel of Yahweh with an entity called "a satan."

Satan is sometimes identified in the Bible with Lucifer, a defiant angel who was cast out of heaven.

> How art thou fallen from heaven, O Lucifer, son of the morning! How art thou cut down to the ground, which didst weaken the nations.[63]

---

62 *The Bible*, Numbers 22:22 KJV
63 *The Bible*, Isaiah 14:12 KJV

In the New Testament, the words Satan and "diabolos", meaning "slanderer," are used interchangeably. The three Synoptic Gospels all tell a story about Jesus being tempted by Satan in the wilderness, a passage used to justify the idea of Satan as one who seduces into sin. Jesus used the figure of Satan metaphorically in some of his parables—the Parable of the Sower, the Parable of the Weeds, the Parable of the Sheep and the Goats, and the Parable of the Strong Man.

The mutation of Satan over the centuries is a fascinating example of folkloric drift. He has been called by many names—Beelzebub, Mephistopheles, Baphomet and the Antichrist—and has shape-shifted into many forms such as a horned beast with cloven hooves, a dragon, a goat-headed monster and even a handsome man. Satan is one of the most popular figures in ancient and popular culture.

Satan, however, is clearly a personification of evil that demonstrates humankind's desire to deflect blame for misdeeds on something other itself. None of the beasts imagined as the evil Satan, none of the fanciful tales in which he stars, are logical as fact-based stories. The most recent wisdom tradition clarifies that by Satan…

> … we mean the natural inclinations of the lower nature. This lower nature in man is symbolized as Satan—the evil ego within us, not an evil personality outside.[64]

Demons and Evil Spirits

What then, of evil spirits and demons? The word demon comes from the Greek word daimōn, which means a "supernatural being" or "spirit." From the dawn of time, humans have been frightened by unseen and wicked spirits, perhaps invented as a way to explain the inexplicable and violent world around them. Belief in evil spirits has always been folklorically interwoven with religious views, particularly

---

64 'Abdu'l-Bahá, *Promulgation of Universal Peace*, p.287

in earlier ages when superstition often outweighed rationality. To the Greeks, the word demons referred to both good and bad spirits that held sway over a person's character.

Since evil is more interesting than goodness, however, the term evolved to mean more specialized forms of evil or malevolent spirits that caused disease, madness, or possession. Theologians and demonologists have categorized demons by name, function and even level of authority or power according to vague references in ancient texts.

In Christianity, demons are often associated with fallen angels who followed Satan, the prince of darkness, and became his servants to tempt, accuse, deceive and take possession of humans. The Catholic Church employs exorcists to cast out imagined demons who have taken possession of humans or animals. A small army of private paranormal investigators now offer to provide the same service. Belief in dark, unseen forces has fueled many occult beliefs and practices outside of religion, and sometimes it is mixed into the religious brew that includes witchcraft, necromancy, divination, sorcery and many others. The belief that mental distress is caused by demons, sin or generational curses is commonplace among many evangelical Christian communities.

These beliefs understandably can have both positive and negative outcomes. Spiritual comfort and fellowship is on the positive end of the spectrum, while the withholding of competent medical and psychological aid is on the distant negative end. It would be wrong to diagnose all physical, mental and emotional disorders as due to personal failures or the work of evil spirits or the "will of God." The science that can cure many ailments has been given to us by God and at last discovered by humankind. Science is a gift that can help unveil superstitions and allow humanity to focus on what is truly important—the development of love and unity for all humankind.

The following passages in the Writings of the most recent wisdom tradition are unabashedly clear, underscoring the importance of viewing these topics rationally.

> As to the question of evil spirits, demons and monsters, any references made to them in the Holy Books have symbolic meaning. What is currently known among the public is but sheer superstition.[65]

> ...one must not turn aside from the advice of a competent doctor. It is imperative to consult one even if the patient himself be a well-known and eminent physician. In short, the point is that you should maintain your health by consulting a highly-skilled physician.[66]

Because the Prophet-Founder of the latest wisdom tradition sometimes uses terms that refer to Satan and malevolent spirits, He has clarified that these terms are used metaphorically, as has always been the case in the world's scriptures. He frequently uses the words "Satan" and "Prince of Darkness." He exhorts His followers to "walk not in the paths of the Evil One.[67]" He speaks of the "manifestations of the Evil Whisperer, who whispers in men's breasts.[68]" But a careful study in context shows that He uses these colorful terms to dramatize His teaching that Satanic impulses come from the "Satan within us[69]," which only we can conquer.

In our opinion, a rational view holds that the world has no such supernatural characters at work because evil does not independently exist.

> Evil consists merely in non-existence. For example, death is the absence of life: When man is no longer sustained by the power of life, he dies. Darkness is the absence of light: When light is no more, darkness reigns. Light is a positively existing thing, but darkness

---

65 *Lights of Guidance*, p. 513.
66 *Lights of Guidance*
67 Bahá'u'lláh, *Gleanings*, p. 126
68 Bahá'u'lláh, *Prayers and Meditations*, p. 233
69 Bahá'u'lláh, *The Kitáb-i-Íqán*, p. 112

> has no positive existence; it is merely its absence. Likewise, wealth is a positively existing thing but poverty is merely its absence.[70]

In other words, we have no evil forces to blame for our errors. "The Devil made me do it," comedian Flip Wilson famously suggested. But he was only joking. As humans, we are fully capable of messing up without the manipulation of malevolent spirits, though blaming the Devil is certainly tempting at times.

Heaven and Hell

If there is a logical way of comprehending evil, sin, Satan and demons, can heaven and hell also be understood rationally? What role do they play in this cosmic story made rational by the most recent wisdom tradition?

If there were a literal and malicious spirit called Satan who could unleash a legion of wicked demons to do his handiwork, they would require a dwelling place, and so folklore delivered one—a literal place we often call Hell. Fear and punishment have always been used as instruments of social manipulation, and Hell became both a home for the source of evil as well as for the damned who succumbed to its temptations. The concept of Hell, like that of Satan and demons, has changed enormously over time, and different religions and cultures have various beliefs about the afterlife and the fate of the wicked.

In the Hebrew Bible, there is no clear concept of a place of eternal torment for sinners. The Hebrew term *Sheo* describes a dark and gloomy realm to which all the dead—good and bad—are delivered. The term *Gehenna* (literally the valley of Hinnom) originally referred to a place outside Jerusalem where trash and corpses were burned. Later, the name for this place of cremation became a metaphor for God's fiery judgment on sinners.

---

70 'Abdu'l-Bahá, *Some Answered Questions*, Part 5, "Miscellaneous Subjects"; 74, "On Good and Evil."

The New Testament authors, who wrote in Greek, translated the Hebrew word *Sheol* into *Hades*, which handily referred to their god of the underworld in Greek mythology. *Hades* eventually became known as a place where the souls of the dead were sent to be judged.

Wicked souls were sent to Tartarus, a dark abyss in which they were tormented, sometimes by fire, according to the severity of their sins. Righteous souls were sent to Elysium, a blissful paradise. The term *Gehenna* is used to indicate the final destination of damned souls after resurrection and their last judgment. It is described as a place where "the fire never goes out[71]" and "there will be weeping and gnashing of teeth.[72]"

In the fourteenth century, an Italian writer named Dante Alighieri wrote an epic poem—the first part of a longer work called *The Divine Comedy*—telling the story of his odyssey through Hell guided by the Roman poet Virgil. In Hell, he comes upon nine populated circles, each circle corresponding to a type of sin. The sinners in these circles are punished according to the principle of contrapasso—poetic justice—which dictates that their punishments must fit their crimes.

Dante illustrated his poem with frightening and grotesque depictions of torture, and these graphical images became engraved in the public's mind, eventually becoming the de facto illustration of the torments of hell. Rationally, this damned place called Hell makes no sense as it proposes that souls, which are spiritual entities, could be subjected to physical tortures. But the concept of Hell has for centuries frightened millions of people who took the illustrations literally.

The Greek concept of Elysium, a paradise for righteous souls, evolved into the idea of heaven, a concept for which there are as many interpretations as there are people on earth. The concept of heaven as a physical place also makes no sense because after death, if there is

---

71   *The Bible*, Mark 9:43, KJV
72   *The Bible*, Matthew 13:42, KJV

an afterlife, it cannot coexist with our physical bodies. Anyway, who would want those decrepit bodies?

A question remains. If there is no Hell to discourage us from sinning, and no heaven to reward us for righteous behavior, why would anyone ever comply with the demands of righteous rules and regulations? How could we ever achieve an ever-advancing civilization? Would we not lapse into anarchy?

The most recent wisdom tradition explains that when human beings...

> are illumined by the rays of the Sun of Truth and endowed with every human virtue, they reckon this as the greatest reward and regard it as the true paradise. In like manner, they consider spiritual punishment... to consist in subjection to the world of nature; in being veiled from God; in ignorance and unawareness; in engrossment with covetous desires; in absorption in animal vices; in being marked by evil attributes, such as falsehood, tyranny, and iniquity; in attachment to worldly things... all of which they reckon to be the greatest of torments and punishments...[73]

This is not to say that as spiritual beings we will not experience an afterlife, just not the one depicted in evolving religious folklore. Our latest wisdom tradition explains that we cannot comprehend the world in which we enter upon physical death any more than a child in the womb can conceive life in this physical world. Neither we nor the infant has any useful frame of reference. And yet, we are cautioned to not be so concerned with the next life that our physical existence here is reduced to being merely a waiting room.

That heaven is not a physical place, or even something that human minds can fathom, was made clear in the Writings of the most recent wisdom tradition. In one passage, answering the question of

---

73 'Abdu'l-Bahá, *Some Answered Questions*, p. 224

what Jesus meant when he said "the Son of man is in heaven," and about His birth said He had come from heaven, the Writings explain...

> ...Consider how it is said that the Son of man is in heaven, even though at that time Christ was dwelling upon the earth. Consider likewise that it explicitly says that Christ came from heaven, although He came from the womb of Mary and His body was born of her. It is therefore clear that the assertion that the Son of man came down from heaven has a mystical rather than a literal meaning, and is a spiritual rather than a material event... And His ascension to heaven, likewise, is spiritual and not material in nature... for among other things the ascension of Christ in a physical body to the material heavens is contrary to the mathematical sciences.[74]

If heaven is a spiritual reality and not a physical place, heaven can be thought of as nearness to God and the opposite, hell, can be thought of as separation from God. A much-loved Christian hymn is entitled, "Nearer My God to Thee." What could be more rewarding? Certainly not streets of gold, but rather to be close to God with the fullness of renewed life, energy raised to a Divine degree, and exaltation over the limitations of time and space?

> **The wealth of the next world consists in nearness to God.**[75]

> **Know thou of a truth that the soul, after its separation from the body, will continue to progress until it attaineth the presence of God, in a state and condition which neither the revolution of ages and centuries, nor the changes and chances of this world, can alter.**[76]

---

74 'Abdu'l-Bahá, *Some Answered Questions*
75 'Abdu'l-Bahá, Some Answered Questions
76 Bahá'u'lláh, *Gleanings from the Writings of Bahá'u'lláh*, LXXXI

Above all things, heaven is reunion with God.

> Thy Paradise is My love; thy heavenly home, reunion with Me. Enter therein and tarry not.[77]

> For the true lover desireth naught save reunion with his beloved and the seeker hath no goal but to attain unto the object of his quest.[78]

Morality

Acceptance of the oneness of humanity leads directly to the concept of morality, which in simple terms refers to a set of principles that differentiate between behaviors that are right and wrong or good and bad for both individuals and societies. The purpose of making these distinctions is to assist societies of great diversity to live in unity and security with minimal social disruption and injustice.

Since most moral codes by which individuals live are largely based on the religious doctrines in which they are entangled, the variation of these religious, moral and traditional beliefs can become a great source of disunity, which supports the destructive process of disintegration. In the past, religious beliefs gave rise to cultural standards of behavior, which later became the standards of morality. Rationally, however, we can see that morality is more than just cultural norms since individuals can change cultures by migrating from one place to another, adapting to new social environments while still maintaining their original moral standards. In a fluid and global society, when there is no basic agreement on something so fundamental as rules of conduct, developing a peaceful and tranquil world is impossible.

---

77 Bahá'u'lláh, *The Hidden Words of Bahá'u'lláh*
78 Bahá'u'lláh, *Summons of the Lord of Hosts*

A rational solution of conflicting moral codes and the resulting disunity is to look for Divine guidance because...

> ...the Manifestation of God [Prophet] only gives us teachings and instructions designed for our good and protection...[79]

Sometimes, acting in a moral manner means individuals must sacrifice their own short-term interests or desires to benefit society. Prohibitions against infidelity, for example—which is generally accompanied by a lack of truthfulness—usually causes disunity and upheaval not only between the spouses but between many layers of family members,. It can disrupt the family unit, which is the basis of organized societies.

For individuals, the oneness of humankind demands a morality set up for humans who are equal, sacred and mirrors of divine attributes. Each individual is loved and dignified in this vision of humanity, thus acting in a moral fashion is not so much dependent on punishments for misbehavior but on consequences that are the natural outcome of behaving in an unsuitable way. Both natural consequences and prescribed punishments can be foreseen. Morality is thus also based on pure intentions; how one adapts to new situations; one's commitment to the principles of equality and unity; and a preference for the wellbeing of others over one's self. Essentially, this morality is based on love.

For societies in general, moral behavior requires structures and laws to hold nations accountable for immoral actions. Of course, the more the individuals in these societies appreciate the oneness of humanity and behave in keeping with the morality of love, the greater will be society's moral behavior.

The philosophy of natural law is based on the concept that there is an eternal and unchangeable law that encompasses all peoples of

---

79   Shoghi Effendi, *Unfolding Destiny*, p. 444.

all ages, a law that is in accord with right reason and shared by all human beings. This sounds like the spiritual principles that are common to all the world's great wisdom traditions. Plato, Aristotle, Thomas Aquinas, Leibniz and many other great thinkers concluded that the laws and definitions regarding the categories of good, evil, just and unjust—like the immutable laws of mathematics—would be just as valid if God did not exist. In this view, the Prophets of the great wisdom traditions revealed and summarized for us as spiritual principles the natural laws of morality that have always existed, truths that can be recognized by human reason.

> All the Prophets have come to promote divine bestowals, to found the spiritual civilization and teach the principles of morality.[80]

Personal and Collective Acts of Violence

In our modern age, perhaps nothing illustrates the decline of traditional morals and the resulting sickness of society more than the savaging of our world by violent acts. Violence shows something is wrong with society just as predictably as a rising temperature indicates a person's body is ailing. What is most horrifying, however, is not that violence erupts so often but that it is becoming customary and expected. Only major acts of violence now produce collective gasps. Most acts seem trivial, banal, hardly worthy of attention. We have become desensitized so quickly that only the most dramatic and brutal acts rouse our emotions.

Hate crimes involving violence are particularly troubling. We have seen people of religious groups killed and wounded in their churches. Racist acts of violence by both citizens and law enforcement. Political violence directed at governmental leaders and electoral processes. Inter-gang violence over turf and drugs. A big increase in

---

80 'Abdu'l-Bahá, *The Promulgation of Universal Peace*

rapes often resulting in murder. At its core, violence is a moral issue that results from hate, anger, resentment, desire for power and lack of respect for others and their beliefs. The proliferation of guns can turn minor disputes into killing sprees. It is hard to imagine anything more disunifying for society than acts of violence.

As a society's values and morals deteriorate, its cohesion and unity begins to perish. Society cannot advance and will regress if obligations of its members to each other disappear, if there is no spontaneous willingness to obey the law or moral code, if members forego the temptations of ill-gotten gain at the expense of others, if society yields to hedonism and egotism and loses its ability to share and sacrifice. We have beheld in previous decades the shameful abuses of religious leaders on the least of their parishioners—the children. Rather than rise to the call of spiritual guidance and leadership, some clergy have instead chosen to abandon morality and prey upon those in their care.

> Any religion which is not a cause of love and unity is no religion. All the holy prophets were as doctors to the soul; they gave prescriptions for the healing of mankind; thus any remedy that causes disease does not come from the great and supreme Physician.

Many historians have pointed out that humanity most likely is less violent than it was two hundred, five hundred or a thousand years ago. It may be that our expectations for a less violent world have been rising, our tools for inflicting damage have improved and our knowledge of violent acts has increased dramatically. In this sense, perhaps, we can see signs of humanity coming of age ever so slowly despite our capacities for causing harm.

One of the "supreme Physician's" most potent prescriptions for the healing of humankind is morality—if we would only read and follow the instructions. Is this not rational thinking?

Self-Degradation

Our latest wisdom tradition stated that infants were born noble—free of sin and debasement. Self-degradation is thus a personal choice or the consequence of bad judgement.

> O Son of Spirit! Noble have I created thee, yet thou hast abased thyself.[81]

For many, the pursuit of physical and material pleasure has led to a fall from this noble beginning. An old axiom sums up this obsession with personal pleasure: "If it feels good, do it." Rational thinking would likely advise that some things that feel good are often harmful to oneself or others. Another saying advises: "Life's too short, so make the most of it." The ambiguity of "making the most of it" is often interpreted as "do what brings you the most pleasure" rather than "make the biggest contribution to the most people." This advice ignores an individual's considerable responsibilities to family, community and the world. The chase to achieve one's material desires.

The insatiable search for personal pleasure and enjoyment has led to the downfall of countless rulers, famous celebrities and many other people throughout history and society who ended up in a cycle of addiction, self-destruction, debasement and suicide. Certainly, there is no harm in enjoying oneself and experiencing happiness and joy, but when personal pleasure becomes hedonism or when materialism engulfs one's life and harms others, it can become toxic to oneself and society.

> Desire and passion, like two unmanageable horses, have wrested the reins of control… and are galloping madly in the wilderness. This is the cause of the degradation of the world of humanity. This is the cause

---

81   Baha'u'llah, *The Hidden Words*, p. 9.

> of its retrogression into the appetites and passions of the animal kingdom. Instead of divine advancement we find sensual captivity and debasement of heavenly virtues of the soul. By devotion to the carnal, mortal world human susceptibilities sink to the level of animalism.[82]

Among the problems that human beings face is confusion between happiness and pleasure. To some extent, past discussion of this topic has been limited by cultural taboos and religious traditions that frown on many things that bring sensory pleasure. In some cultures, listening to music or dancing is still forbidden, labeled as the "work of the devil." Even rhythmically clapping hands is interpreted in some quarters as making music and is therefore punishable. We are not sure about whistling—is that happiness or pleasure?

The Internet has unbridled these unmanageable horses by bringing pornography, one example of self-degradation, into the homes of any seeker of sexual self-gratification. Consuming porn is a global, escalating epidemic and can be addictive and destructive to family life. No one today is immune from its effects because most people have friends and loved ones who regularly watch porn. The Internet over the past two decades has provided global, unrestricted (except for minors) distribution of pornography into our homes, offices and onto our phones—which makes it available everywhere we go. In 2023, the eleventh most popular website in the world was a pornography site. Though prurient material has been around forever, pornography is a uniquely twenty-first century issue. This is one reason that religion in our ever-changing world requires periodic updates.

Should we not ask what has happened to the nobility of humankind, and to where moral rectitude has retreated which previously had been taught by earlier religious beliefs? The alarming deterioration of moral standards throughout the world is highlighted

---

82 'Abdu'l-Bahá, *The Promulgation of Universal Peace*.

by many recent developments: a loosening of the sacred bonds of marriage; overlooked covenants between individuals; inordinate obsession and craving for pleasure and diversion; slackening of parental control of children; abundance of lies and deceit in public discourse.

> ... Every age hath its own problem, and every soul its particular aspiration. The remedy the world needeth in its present-day afflictions can never be the same as that which a subsequent age may require.[83]

A few decades ago, viewing pornography was mainly seen as a shameful act that betrayed a personal moral failure. Today, behaviors previously seen only in porn are now common in art, music, television, movies, games, books, magazines, comedy, fashion and other forms of expression. As a result, countless people of all ages (children as young as eight have been diagnosed as "problem users") are finding themselves unable to break their addiction to porn, many people are living in isolation because of its effects, marriages and families are falling apart as a direct result and many young people are finding it difficult to engage in healthy dating and mating.

This current crisis of pornography logically requires us to move into a new era of sexual healing and maturity, which in turn can free us from harmful addictions so we can behave as rational human beings. If our vision of the future is a spiritually and socially maturing civilization, is it not logical that our collective sexual maturation should be a part of this constructive process? The sexual violence, sexism and ego-satisfying pleasure celebrated in pornography is today a fundamental part of the parallel destructive process.

> ... man should know his own self and recognize that which leadeth unto loftiness or lowliness, glory or abasement, wealth or poverty...[84]

---

83 Baha'u'llah, *Gleanings from the Writings of Baha'u'llah*, p. 213.
84 Baha'u'llah, *Tablets of Baha'u'llah*, p. 35.

> Thy generous Lord will... forgive thy sins and transform them into goodly deeds.[85]

Happiness

While some argue against the overt quest for pleasure and use moral laws to prevent achieving it, no one argues against the pursuit of happiness. In recent years, various institutions have begun to quantify happiness scientifically based on material measurements. For over ten years, the United Nations has funded a global study called the World Happiness Report. According to one of the authors for 2022, Jeffrey Sachs, "The lesson from the report in these ten years is that generosity among people and honesty among governments are critical to well-being."[86]

According to researcher Dr. Robert H. Lustig, Professor emeritus of Pediatric Endocrinology at the University of California, San Franciso[87], happiness and pleasure are two different concepts caused by the production of two distinct biochemicals in the brain, dopamine and serotonin, that follow distinct neural pathways. Until now, people have not understood the biological differences between happiness and pleasure, therefore they have used these two words almost interchangeably. The differences, however. can be summarized by these seven points:

1. Pleasure is short-lived, whereas happiness is long-lived.
2. Pleasure is visceral (felt within the body), whereas happiness is ethereal (spiritual, not material).
3. Pleasure is taking; happiness is giving.
4. Pleasure can be fulfilled with substances; happiness cannot be fulfilled by using substances.

---

85 'Abdu'l-Bahá, *Selections from the Writings of Abdu'l-Baha*, p. 164.
86 www.prudentpressagency.com, 2022.
87 Lustig, YouTube presentation recorded by UCTV, September 7, 2017.

5. Pleasure is experienced alone; happiness is experienced with groups.
6. Extreme pleasure leads to addiction to substances or behaviors. Happiness, however, can never be addictive—there can never be too much happiness.
7. Feelings of pleasure is the result of *dopamine*; a sense of happiness is the result of *serotonin*. Both are biochemical neurotransmitters. Dopamine excites neurons, but if they are excited too much and too frequently, they tend to die. As a defense mechanism, neurons reduce the number of receptors to the stimulant in an effort to lessen neuron destruction. This results in a greater need for the stimulant to obtain the same effect as previously felt, resulting in addiction. As more and more stimulant is required, more neurons are destroyed until finally it is not possible to obtain the same "rush" that was experienced before. On the other hand, serotonin has an inhibitory effect on neurons. As a result, serotonin promotes contentment or a feeling of happiness.

This scientific study substantiates the biochemical differences between happiness and pleasure, confirming that happiness comes from within, whereas pleasure is affected by external stimuli or forces. This also explains the operation of advertising, which tries to convince us to spend money on things that we may like but do not truly need. In the end, the products may give us some pleasure and cause us to want increasing doses of that pleasure but cannot deliver true happiness or contentment.

Materialism, takes a toll on the mental health of individuals and their families. A greater dependence on "things" that deliver pleasure can cause some people to become addicted to shopping, for example, as a way to produce a constant flow of pleasures that never truly satisfies us or produces the deep happiness we seek. When so much thought and attention is devoted to obtaining temporary pleasures, the spiritual development of our rational soul, which ultimately leads to long-lasting happiness, can be neglected. The true purpose of morality, then, is not to limit pleasure but to make more room for the development of true happiness. The pursuit of pleasure places ever greater demands on us to enjoy ever diminishing returns. Should we not, then, invest more heavily where the returns are greatest?

Chapter 5:
Science and Religion

A Failure to Agree

Ever since humans sensed that something bigger and outside of themselves must be present in the world and discovered the first facts about how their material world operated, religion and science have been mortal combatants for supremacy in the minds of those who inhabit our planet. Perhaps the tension between these two domains of knowledge arose because one is intangible and the other is tangible. Humans of earlier times—accustomed to simple binary choices such as good or bad—became either predominantly superstitious or materially pragmatic. We don't really know which epiphany came first or how the conflict began, but for centuries a prevailing world view has been that science and religion are contradictory terms that no amount of negotiation can resolve.

Historically, this disagreement has been so deep and intense and the battle lines so hardened that the disharmony has proven difficult to eradicate. As scientific knowledge has expanded and religious knowledge has become more informed by science, the two domains have been infringing on the proclaimed territory of each other. Moral and ethical issues, once the province of religion, are now demanding solutions by scientists more accustomed to the empirical world of measurable experiments and observable behavior. Scientific evidence contradictory to many literal religious beliefs is demanding a defense from theologians more comfortable with philosophical and spiritual matters. These overlapping jurisdictions are creating competition and friction, though there are a range of nuanced views.

The core truth is that both domains of knowledge are necessary for the advancement of civilization.

> ...religion without science soon degenerates into superstition and fanaticism, while science without religion becomes the tool of crude materialism...[88]

Models for Conflict

No meaningful discussion about this matter can occur without understanding the classic paradigms or models within which most arguments reside.

1. *The Conflict (or Warfare) Model* in which science aggressively opposes religion and religion aggressively opposes science.
2. *The Replacement Model* in which science supplants religion altogether.
3. *The Independence Model* in which science avoids consultation with religion and vice versa.
4. *The Reconciliation Model* in which science engages with religion and religion reciprocates.

These fundamental frameworks illustrate the futility of most disputes about science vs. religion that do not identify which branch of science and which religion or sect are having the dispute. Religions

---

88 Universal House of Justice, "Non-Involvement in Partisan Politics," March 2, 2013.

have different views about science and many scientists are deeply religious. A reasonable summary of the problem, of which both sides share the blame, is offered by the latest wisdom tradition:

> The outcome of all this dissension is the belief of many cultured men that religion and science are contradictory terms, that religion needs no powers of reflection, and should in no wise be regulated by science, but must of necessity be opposed, the one to the other. The unfortunate effect of this is that science has drifted apart from religion, and religion has become a mere blind… following of the precepts of certain religious teachers, who insist on their own favourite dogmas being accepted even when they are contrary to science. This is foolishness, for it is quite evident that science is the light, and, being so, religion truly so-called does not oppose knowledge.[89]

True Religion Is Not a Cause of Discord

Our newest wisdom tradition distinguishes between true [Divine] religion revealed by Messengers of God and blind faith resulting in religious superstition, a byproduct of human ignorance and corruption.

> Divine religion is not a cause for discord and disagreement. If religion becomes the source of antagonism and strife, the absence of religion is to be preferred. Religion is meant to be the quickening life of the body politic; if it be the cause of death to humanity, its non-existence would be a blessing and benefit to man.[90]

---

89 'Abdu'l-Bahá, *Paris Talks*
90 'Abdu'l-Bahá, *The Promulgation of Universal Peace*, p. 117

Religion and science need each other to fully develop a more advanced civilization. Neither can do it alone, and neither can survive alone without self-destruction. Society without religion does not have the motivation or the skills to develop virtues and noble character. Without the positive influence of religion, society can become more humanitarian and promote materialistic idealism, but this unlikely will promote compassion and altruism as well as religion can in its ideal form. And yet we must acknowledge that great cruelties and suffering have been imposed on humankind in the name of religion.

> Religious fanaticism and hatred are a world-devouring fire, whose violence none can quench.[91]

Religion without science and rational thinking risks losing its way and descends into nonsense unworthy of serious consideration.

> Religion must stand the analysis of reason. It must agree with scientific fact and proof so that science will sanction religion and religion fortify science. Both are indissolubly welded and joined in reality. If statements and teachings of religion are found to be unreasonable and contrary to science, they are outcomes of superstition and imagination.[92]

Science enables humanity to separate fact from conjecture and its capabilities. It observes, accurately measures and rigorously tests ideas and theories that have helped us build a useful understanding of physical reality, human conduct and societal life.

> Science is the first emanation from God toward man. All created things embody the potentiality of material perfection, but the power of intellectual investigation

---

91 Bahá'u'lláh, *Epistle to the Son of the Wolf*, p. 15.
92 'Abdu'l-Bahá, *The Promulgation of Universal Peace*, p. 175-176.

> and scientific acquisition is a higher virtue specialized to man alone.[93]

While there are many skeptics about both science and religion, some have noticed the ascendancy of science over religious influence around the world. The decline of religion is largely due to the endless disputes between the followers of different faiths.

> Irreligion has conquered religion. The cause of the chaotic condition lies in the differences among the religions and finds its origin in the animosity and hatred existing between sects and denominations... Owing to strife and contention among themselves, the religions are being weakened and vanquished... enmity, strife and recrimination prevail among them... if necessary they shed each other's blood.[94]

For those who question the value or relevance of religion in a modern, science-oriented world, the following quotations provides a response for consideration by comparing "material civilization" (science-based) and Divine civilization (augmented by religion).

> Material civilization is like a lamp-glass. Divine civilization is the lamp itself and the glass without the light is dark. Material civilization is like the body. No matter how infinitely graceful, elegant and beautiful it may be, it is dead. Divine civilization is like the spirit, and the body gets its life from the spirit, otherwise it becomes a corpse... Without the spirit the world of mankind is lifeless, and without this light the world of mankind is in utter darkness.

---

93   'Abdu'l-Bahá, *The Promulgation of Universal Peace*, p. 21.
94   'Abdu'l-Bahá, *The Promulgation of Universal Peace*, p. 161.

Reasons People Mistrust Science

There are many contemporary arguments between religious people who dispute inconvenient or disagreeable scientific facts and those who favor science over the religious beliefs or superstitions of their adversaries. Most of these conflicts are unworthy of intelligent people because they are irrational, often on both sides.

> How can a man believe to be a fact that which science has proved to be impossible? If he believes in spite of his reason, it is rather ignorant superstition than faith.[95]

As discussed below, there are numerous reasons why some people, many of them religious by disposition, are anti-science:

Suspicions about Experts and "Elites"

During the COVID-19 pandemic, legions of people turned against Dr. Anthony Fauci, at that time director of the National Institute of Allergy and Infectious Diseases (NIAID), who oversaw the nation's pandemic response. Yes, the overwhelming vehemence cast upon him was fueled by unfounded conspiracy theories and massive social media protests, but the tinder for the wildfire was already in place.

Before the pandemic, there was already widespread partisan cynicism about elite institutions like the CDC and "cold and unfeeling" scientists in general who often spoke in a secret scientific language that no non-scientist could understand. Also, many people remembered when Tennessee politicians with robust evangelical Christian backing tried to ban the teaching of evolution in public schools. The arguments supported by scientists were seen as strongly hostile and insulting to Christian teachings, values and beliefs. The highly adversarial courtroom process did not allow for a friendlier consultation of the issue and the bitter sentiments spilled over to Christian communities throughout the country.

---

95 'Abdu'l-Bahá, *Paris Talks*.

During the COVID-19 crisis, the credibility of scientists was further weakened when a series of confusing health recommendations were made by the scientific community and some masking requirements were even withdrawn. The public was told initially that no one needed to wear masks, then that the masks were needed but supplies were short because ND95 masks were prioritized for healthcare workers. Then cloth masks were deemed unsuitable and everyone had to wear ND95 masks. The recommendations changed because new information became available—that is how science works—but the public saw science as unreliable and even likely operating as pawns of imaginary dark forces dictating policy.

Research by Brown University and Microsoft AI Health showed that by April of 2022, nearly 319,000 deaths could have been averted if all adults had been vaccinated, and the main reason for refusing vaccination was lack of confidence in the science despite scientist assurances.[96]

Social Identities

Most people identify with various social groups, which were explained in "Chapter 3: The Oneness of a Diverse Humanity." In some cases, perceived biases or injustices committed against one of their groups causes many in that group to dislike the perpetrators even if they were not injured themselves. For example, many who identify with American Blacks or Indigenous Peoples are wary of medical scientists because other group members in the past were subjected to often hateful experiments without their knowledge.

Because many evangelical Christian televangelists and preachers frightened their flocks with unfounded stories of COVID-19 vaccine perils and scolded congregants for a lack of faith if they were vaccinated, many evangelicals deflected their leaders' wrath onto the scientific establishment. Religions and sects that held fast to doctrines that prescribe prayer as the only remedy for physical

---

96 NPR at https://n.pr/3KFyvZG.

ailments as well as creationists who believe the Genesis creation story is a factual historical record of God's handiwork are often vocal skeptics of science. Social identity dynamics play a major role in the rise of false and irrational conspiracy theories such as the claim that COVID-19 vaccines secretly contain microchips. This is a good example of calumny, the use of a false story to taint a good concept and cause many to blindly believe the falsehood.

Calumny is not a modern technique. It was also used against Jesus and other Divine Educators.

> In the day of Christ, Annas and Caiaphas inflamed the Jewish people against Him and the learned doctors of Israel joined together to resist His Power. All sorts of calumnies were circulated against Him. The Scribes and Pharisees conspired to make the people believe Him to be a liar, an apostate, and a blasphemer. They spread these slanders throughout the whole Eastern world against Christ, and caused Him to be condemned to a shameful death![97]

Invalidating a World View

The most infamous example of a reason for denying science—that a scientific fact overturns an existing world view—is the rejection of a discovery by Copernicus that the Earth rotates around the sun. Contrary to popular belief, the Catholic Church at first accepted the astronomer's heliocentric theory but surrendered to a wave of Protestant accusations of heresy to defend the false belief that the sun rotated around the Earth, which had been observable "common knowledge" for more than four centuries.

After Catholics joined the Protestant opposition, they were abandoned in their anti-science position as Protestant's eventually accepted the findings of new evidence that Copernicus was right.

---

97 'Abdu'l-Bahá, *Paris Talks*.

The Catholic Church remained anti-Copernican until the ban on his views was lifted in 1822.

This long-fought war shows that people have difficulty when they are confronted with the "cognitive dissonance" of conflicting information. They are comfortable thinking in concrete terms consistent with what they have always believed and will cling to grossly erroneous beliefs even when presented with strong evidence. This may be why "fake news" and misinformation is so pervasive and hard to counter.

Qualified Truth

Many studies have found that most people prefer clear answers to questions. The fuzzier or more conditional the answers, the more people tune out or fail to comprehend. Because of the complex nature of their work, scientists seldom have black-and-white conclusions to share, so many have become masters of an epistemic style of communicating. An epistemic conclusion is one that may be true if certain conditions or constraints are also true. An example is: "If the low front continues to move westward at its present rate, it might rain tomorrow." When the epistemic communication style of a scientific expert does not match the receiving style of an audience member, the message usually doesn't get through.

This means that the messages of people who communicate in nuanced and qualified ways will be dismissed if the recipients think chiefly in a concrete, black-and-white manner. We can see this happening in discussions about climate change, which is often presented in abstract terms disconnected with the daily lives of the audience. The way that scientists talk to lay audiences, then, often undercuts the authority of their conclusions. Too often, scientists hedge their findings to avoid overclaiming certainty of preliminary or inconclusive conclusions to recipients who cannot tolerate uncertainty. In general, scientists are ill-equipped to present scientific truth as it is currently known.

A Common Goal but Different Methods

Mistrust does not mean disharmony. It is possible that both science and religion are in pursuit of the same thing—the truth of reality. If God created the universe and everything in it, then God by definition created science and all its laws. He also must have created all the spiritual laws that govern the world but science cannot yet see or measure. If there is a dispute between science and religion, then it must be due to a lack of sufficient knowledge about one or the other; there is no other plausible explanation. Either the scientific facts are incomplete or misunderstood, or the religious concepts are likewise lacking depth of knowledge or misinterpretation. The one thing that both sides can assuredly agree upon is that our knowledge of both science and religion is extraordinarily limited.

> **Make every effort to acquire the advanced knowledge of the day, and strain every nerve to carry forward the divine civilization.**[98]

We can also agree, perhaps, that science and religion complement each other.

> **There is no contradiction between true religion and science. When a religion is opposed to science it becomes mere superstition: that which is contrary to knowledge is ignorance... If religion were in harmony with science and they walked together, much of the hatred and bitterness now bringing misery to the human race would be at an end.**[99]

The biggest agreement between science and religion, however, is on the need to search for truth, for reality, whatever it may be.

---

98 'Abdu'l-Bahá, from a Tablet translated from the Persian and quoted on http://bahai.org.

99 'Abdu'l-Bahá, *Paris Talks*.

Scientists may suspect that people of religion are more interested in defending their beliefs about reality than exploring reality for its deeper and more accurate truths. People active in religion may suspect scientists of losing objectivity when considering spiritual matters or harboring biases they would never allow in the scientific process; they may be right in some cases. In its essence, however, the authors believe that both will agree with the following advice:

> If a man would succeed in his search after truth, he must, in the first place, shut his eyes to all the traditional superstitions of the past.[100]

Each of these organized disciplines, however—science and religion—have peculiar shortcomings that make it meaningless to examine certain aspects of reality. Empirical facts about morals, ethics or values do not exist, so the scientific method cannot test them for truth or falsity. Knowledge can be tested but wisdom cannot. Religion, on the other hand, can provide humanity with a code of ethics and morals to improve life for all, but cannot help calculate the distance of Earth from the Sun.

> Religion and science are the two wings upon which man's intelligence can soar into the heights, with which the human soul can progress.[101]

> A bird has two wings; it cannot fly with one. Material and spiritual science are the two wings of human uplift and attainment. Both are necessary—one the natural, the other supernatural; one material, the other divine.[102]

---

100 'Abdu'l-Bahá, *Paris Talks*.
101 'Abdu'l-Bahá, *Paris Talks*.
102 'Abdu'l-Bahá, *The Promulgation of World Peace*.

Chapter 6: Prejudice

A Holistic System of Maturation

The spiritual principles we have been describing have great value when considered individually, but when combined, the whole is worth far more than the sum of the parts. Each principle is necessary for the entire apparatus to make sense and work efficiently.

The principles of the oneness of God, of humanity and of religion are the foundation, we have been told, of a system of understandings and actions that will help usher in a future civilization that is more united and peaceful. The three onenesses, if accepted by a critical mass of individuals, create a new paradigm that allows for additional principles to take root in the consciousness of humanity. The first of these is to recognize the fundamental destructive power of prejudice and the need to uproot it.

> A new religious principle is that prejudice and fanaticism—whether sectarian, denominational, patriotic or political—are destructive to the foundation of human solidarity; therefore, man should release himself from such bonds in order that the oneness of the world of humanity may become manifest.[103]

---
103 'Abdu'l-Bahá, *The Promulgation of Universal Peace*.

All Prejudices are Destructive

The most recent wisdom tradition has stated firmly that prejudices of all kinds are corrosive to human relationships and societies in general.

> All prejudices, whether of religion, race, politics or nation, must be renounced, for these prejudices have caused the world's sickness. It is a grave malady which, unless arrested, is capable of causing the destruction of the whole human race. Every ruinous war, with its terrible bloodshed and misery, has been caused by one or other of these prejudices.[104]

Prejudices, which are hardened mindsets usually rooted in misinformation, are like noxious, invasive species of weeds that greedily spread throughout the land and resist our best efforts to eradicate them.

> As long as these prejudices prevail, the world of humanity will not have rest. For a period of 6,000 years… humanity has not been free from war, strife, murder and bloodthirstiness. In every period war… was due to either religious prejudice, racial prejudice, political prejudice or patriotic prejudice. It has therefore been ascertained and proved that all prejudices are destructive of the human edifice. As long as these prejudices persist, the struggle for existence must remain dominant, and bloodthirstiness and rapacity continue.[105]

In all cases, by diminishing other people for a variety of reasons, prejudices work to selfishly inflate our own self-esteem by comparison. The more unworthy or defective someone else is, the greater is one's own worth.

---

104 'Abdu'l-Bahá, *Paris Talks*.
105 'Abdu'l-Bahá, "First Tablet to the Hague," 17 December 1919.

> Let us therefore be humble, without prejudices, preferring others' good to our own! Let us never say, "I am a believer but he is an infidel," "I am near to God, whilst he is an outcast." ... Therefore let us help all who are in need of any kind of assistance.[106]

Today, when so many people are suffering from a crisis of identity—gender confusion, migration to new countries and cultures, multiracialism, political extremism, et cetera—there are more ways than ever to recategorize and divide humanity. Prejudices can find easy targets almost everywhere.

> The crisis of identity is directly related to the spread of prejudice. Today, prejudices of all sorts are surging around the world, infecting the consciousness of millions and despoiling them of their energies. They are polarizing societies at a time when unity is most vital to resolving local, national, and global challenges that seem intractable.[107]

For those who are sincere in making a personal search for truth through rational thinking, identifying and eliminating prejudices from oneself is a good place to start.

> Man must cut himself free from all prejudice and from the result of his own imagination, so that he may be able to search for truth unhindered. Truth is one in all religions, and by means of it the unity of the world can be realized.[108]

---

106 'Abdu'l-Bahá, *Paris Talks*.
107 Letter from the Universal House of Justice to the Followers of Bahá'u'lláh in the Democratic Republic of the Congo 4 July 2022.
108 'Abdu'l-Bahá, *Paris Talks*.

Causes of Prejudice

There are many types of prejudice, but all of them derive from two common defects in humanity, both of which can be considered root causes:

> ... the root cause of prejudice is ignorance, which can be erased through educational processes that make knowledge accessible to the entire human race, ensuring it does not become the property of a privileged few...[109]

> ... the root cause of prejudice is blind imitation of the past—imitation in religion, in racial attitudes, in national bias, in politics. So long as this aping of the past persisteth, just so long will the foundations of the social order be blown to the four winds, just so long will humanity be continually exposed to direst peril.[110]

These two societal defects are connected but curable, so the development of prejudices is not inevitable. Ignorance, which can be cured through universal education (we will cover this in a later chapter), naturally leads to blind imitation of old, unchallenged beliefs often learned from family and society in general. When challenged objectively, prejudices can be easily dismissed because their foundational facts can be disproven. Most prejudices are simply based on stereotypes ("most Arabs are terrorists", "Muslims worship a false God named Allah"); fear of the differences in others ("those turbans are scary"), overstated competitiveness ("those Mexicans are out to take my job"), stereotypes ("Jews dominate the halls of power at my expense"); conspiracy theories ("Democrats are mostly pedophiles"); misconceptions ("most poor people are lazy"); et cetera.

---

[109] Letter from the Universal House of Justice to the Bahá'ís of Iran 2 March 2013.

[110] 'Abdu'l-Bahá, *Selections from the Writings of 'Abdu'l-Bahá*, p. 202.

There may be cultural similarities and common behaviors among people who share a culture or religion, but there are also widespread individual differences among the people of any culture, ethnic group, race, religion, nation, gender identity, class, language or Zodiac sign. To infer from any such group a member's personal characteristics is prejudicial and potentially a cause of disunity.

> All are the children and servants of God. Why should we be separated by artificial and imaginary boundaries? In the animal kingdom the doves flock together in harmony and agreement. They have no prejudices. We are human and superior in intelligence. Is it befitting that lower creatures should manifest virtues which lack expression in man?[111]

Fanaticism

Most of us harbor prejudices that we fail to recognize because they remain hidden in our subconscious and emerge only in certain circumstances. Generally, these private prejudices are modest in degree and difficult to identify as biases until called out by a third party or exposed by some kind of public behavior or remark. But sometimes prejudices simmer and then come to a boil, bursting out explosively as fanaticism and hatred. Fanaticism is characterized by dogmatic persistence in defending and promoting prejudicial assumptions. It is often fueled by hatred or fear.

> Religious fanaticism and hatred are a world-devouring fire, whose violence none can quench.[112]

When prejudicial assumptions are rooted in superstitious beliefs or conspiracy theories, they provide tinder for the world-devouring

---

111 'Abdu'l-Bahá, *The Promulgation of Universal Peace*.
112 Bahá'u'lláh, *Epistle to the Son of the Wolf*.

fire mentioned earlier. But even the noblest virtues can degenerate into religious fanaticism and bigotry. Religious fanaticism is a blind perversion of allegiance, a pathological excess of the virtues of steadfastness and fortitude. Combined with ignorance and prejudice, it subverts the base of civilization and inspires radical and usually hateful thinking often in the service of political motives or religious ambitions. A well-educated and wise person will always try to learn from others and will never claim to have absolutely correct views since there is always more knowledge to be learned.

The Many Kinds of Prejudice

Religious Prejudice

Of the many kinds of prejudice and discrimination, perhaps none has caused more damage to humanity than religious prejudice. This is extremely discouraging because the purpose of religion is to unite the hearts of humankind.

> ...consider that religion should be the cause of fellowship, otherwise it is fruitless.[113]

Despite the fact that all the world's known wisdom traditions have powerful spiritual truths hidden among the detritus of human interpretations, manmade dogma, mountains of traditions and rituals with forgotten meanings, these religions all originated from the same source. All have the same Divine provenance. And yet, instead of celebrating this commonality, we harbor biases based on the differences.

> Religious prejudice forms a formidable barrier to the progress and well-being of humanity. This prejudice, along with many others, permeates the structures of society and is systematically impressed on individual and collective consciousness. In fact, it is often deliber-

---

113 'Abdu'l-Bahá, "First Tablet to the Hague," 17 December 1919.

> ately fostered and exploited through manipulation and propaganda, using methods that ignore truth and promote self-serving agendas for political or other expediencies.[114]

The principle of the oneness of religion, if generally accepted, has the curative power to unite religions and eliminate—or at least minimize—religious prejudice, a major source of wars and global strife.

> Blessed souls—whether Moses, Jesus, Zoroaster, Krishna, Buddha, Confucius or Muhammad—were the cause of the illumination of the world of humanity. How can we deny such irrefutable proof? How can we be blind to such light? ... We must set aside bias and prejudice. We must abandon the imitations of ancestors and forefathers. We ourselves must investigate reality and be fair in judgment.[115]

Nationalism and Patriotism

Throughout history, nationalism, which leads to patriotism, has been a motivating force for both good and bad. Healthy competition between countries can lead to great achievements and a satisfying sense of citizen pride. Often, however, nationalism becomes so exaggerated that citizens lose sight of their dual role as world citizens. We are, in these times, all affected by global trade. We all live among immigrants from other nations. Humankind is one.

Extreme nationalism can be seen throughout the world today. Just as soccer fans irrationally beat up fans of an opposing team for wearing its colors, nationalism and its accompanying patriotism has degenerated in many places into fanaticism. Rationally, how can we become united as a people if we continue to divide ourselves into

---

[114] Letter to an individual by the Universal House of Justice 27 December 2017.

[115] 'Abdu'l-Bahá, *The Promulgation of Universal Peace.*

small warring tribes? The most recent wisdom tradition explains that national and patriotic prejudice is due to…

> Consider the prejudice of patriotism. This is one globe, one land, one country. God did not divide it into national boundaries. He created all the continents without national divisions. Why should we make such division ourselves? These are but imaginary lines and boundaries. …Man declares a river to be a boundary line between two countries, calling this side French and the other side German, whereas the river was created for both and is a natural artery for all. Is it not imagination and ignorance which impels man to violate the divine intention and make the very bounties of God the cause of war, bloodshed and destruction?[116]

Nationalism and patriotism divide us unnecessarily. Separate nations may be important, but the enmity and disunity that often comes from radical jingoism should be an archaic memory, not a contemporary reality that splits us apart.

Racial and Ethnic Prejudice

Race and ethnicity are concept used to divide sections of the population into categories. Race refers groups of people usually based on physical characteristics. Ethnicity is a way of describing the cultural expression and identification of people from different geographic regions, including their customs, history, language and religion.

In simple terms, race defines physical traits of a group, and ethnicity provides a cultural identification. Race may also be considered something you inherit, whereas ethnicity is something you learn. In terms of prejudices, racial and ethnic biases are quite similar.

The concept of race, and therefore "racism," dates back to the medieval era and became more malignant as a byproduct

---

[116] 'Abdu'l-Bahá, "Talks in Montreal," 1-5 September 1912.

of the American plantation system.[117] Ethnic prejudice, which has plagued societies for a long time, has increased significantly with the enormous influx of refugees and immigrants in many countries. For those who accept it, the principle of the oneness of humankind provides a bulwark against the rising tide of these kinds of prejudices.

> **World order can be founded only on an unshakable consciousness of the oneness of mankind, a spiritual truth which all the human sciences confirm. Anthropology, physiology, psychology, recognize only one human species, albeit infinitely varied in the secondary aspects of life. Recognition of this truth requires abandonment of** prejudice ... **which enables people to consider themselves superior to others.**[118]

Referring to the biblical figure of Adam metaphorically as the first human, not as a historical figure, the newest wisdom tradition boldly highlighted the peril of racism this way:

> ...it is an illusion, a superstition pure and simple! For God created us all of one race. There were no differences in the beginning, for we are all descendants of Adam. In the beginning, also, there were no limits and boundaries between the different lands; no part of the earth belonged more to one people than to another. In the sight of God there is no difference between the various races. Why should man invent such a prejudice?[119]

---

117 https://time.com/5865530/history-race-concept/.
118 The Bahá'i Concept of Equality: Extracts from Letters Written by the Universal House of Justice.
119 'Abdu'l-Bahá, *Paris Talks;* "Part Two: The Fifth Principle- The Abolition of Prejudices."

> Is it reasonable or allowable that a racial prejudice which is not observed by the animal kingdom should be entertained by man?[120]

Ethnic prejudice does not escape scrutiny in this wisdom tradition. Lest there be any doubt that this form prejudice is specifically condemned, the following passage explains that:

> ethnic prejudice can pervade many aspects of collective life and, at its worst, be manifest in recurring cycles of violent conflict. Ethnic prejudice is often driven or exacerbated by prevalent negative social factors... for instance, the effects of ignorance and how it blinds people to the truths that all human beings share the same spiritual essence, are members of one human family, and are inhabitants of one common homeland. Where people are uninformed of the historical processes that have shaped their society, they can tenaciously cling to divisive identities that may have had their roots in an oppressive past. Political partitions between or within countries, which are but human inventions, become bases for the irrational distrust and fear of other groups.[121]

This wisdom tradition explicitly addresses the responsibility of each person:

> For the individual, striving to be free from ethnic prejudice is a profound spiritual duty that no one who claims to be a loyal follower of Bahá'u'lláh can neglect. To

---

120 'Abdu'l-Bahá, *The Promulgation of Universal Peace*, "Talks in Montreal, 1-5," September 1912.

121 Letter from the Universal House of Justice to the Followers of Bahá'u'lláh in the Democratic Republic of the Congo 4 July 2022.

> discriminate against anyone because of ethnicity grievously violates the spirit that animates the Faith.[122]

It is perhaps no coincidence that this most recent wisdom tradition is the second most geographically widespread religion in the world with followers representing over 2,000 ethnic identities.[123]

Political Prejudice

Few kinds of prejudice are so virulent these days as political prejudice. In the US, as well as in many other countries, partisan politics has become so dominated by extremist views that civil discourse and fruitful negotiations have become practically impossible.

> Political prejudice **is equally mischievous, it is one of the greatest causes of bitter strife amongst the children of men. There are people who find pleasure in breeding discord, who constantly endeavor to goad their country into making war upon other nations—and why? They think to advantage their own country to the detriment of all others. They send armies to harass and destroy the land, in order to become famous in the world, for the joy of conquest.**[124]

The partisan part of politics is by definition disunifying, the whole point being to divide and conquer the other side. The latest wisdom tradition describes politics and religion as two separate spheres of human activity that don't mix well.

> Religion is concerned with things of the spirit, politics with things of the world. Religion has to work with the

---

122 Letter from the Universal House of Justice "To the Believers in the Cradle of the Faith" 28 July 2008.
123 https://en.wikipedia.org/wiki/Bah%C3%A1%CA%BC%C3%AD_Faith_by_country
124 'Abdu'l-Bahá, *Paris Talks*.

> world of thought, whilst the field of politics lies with the world of external conditions.[125]

In the US, as evangelical Christians become more closely aligned with conservative political entities, many Christian liberals feel they have lost their home in Christian churches, which often preach racially and ethnically divisive politics from the pulpit. Likewise, the Republican Party's close embrace of exclusionary Christian doctrine encourages many people of color and non-Christian faiths to avoid conservative politics. This divisiveness cannot help achieve the unity of humankind so necessary to universal peace.

The world's newest wisdom tradition stresses the need for participating in government while not affiliating with any political party and voting one's conscience; by participating without partisan identification in civil society and its many discourses; and by obeying the laws of their government. There are many ways to take an active, non-partisan role in improving one's town, city or location.

This new wisdom tradition discourages clergy from becoming de facto political activists or influences.

> Religious teachers should not invade the realm of politics; they should concern themselves with the spiritual education of the people; they should ever give good counsel to men, trying to serve God and humankind; they should endeavor to awaken spiritual aspiration, and strive to enlarge the understanding and knowledge of humanity, to improve morals, and to increase the love for justice.[126]

> Let them willingly subject themselves to every just king, and to every generous ruler be good citizens. Let

---

125 'Abdu'l-Bahá, *Paris Talks*, p. 132.
126 'Abdu'l-Bahá, *Paris Talks*, p. 158.

> them obey the government and not meddle in political affairs, but devote themselves to the betterment of character and behavior, and fix their gaze upon the Light of the world.[127]

There will always be people to work in the political sphere, take political posts and participate in partisan party politics. The world needs more people to focus their efforts on building a new global community. Partisanship can never build unity among people. Only universal love and peace can do this.

Our newest wisdom tradition explains that the world is transitioning from an old set of political rules to another, and that the divisive principles of partisan politics, which is aggressively adversarial, eventually will disappear and in its place we will form a new system that will in time unify the citizens, the nations, and all the contending peoples of the world.

Language Prejudice

Language is human's greatest achievement, and most scientists agree that it is one characteristic that separates humans from animals. Language is an important means of communication between humans and allows for education, complex discourse, explanation of abstract thoughts and ideas, and artistic expression, but it can also be used as a basis for discrimination and injustice. People who speak different languages, accents or dialects may be discriminated against by those who do not share or value their linguistic features.

In judging whether animals use language or not, some researchers define language as communication that shows similarities to human language, such as having a large inventory of signs or vocalizations. Others argue that language requires designators (words that refer to specific objects or concepts such as "dog") and normativity (a set of rules such as grammar that allows usage to be "correct" or "incorrect.")

---

127 'Abdu'l-Bahá, *Selections from the Writings of 'Abdu'l-Bahá*, p. 138.

A study has found that dogs can understand and respond to words, tone of voice and gestures, but there is no evidence that dogs use language as humans do.

Discrimination based on language can be interpersonal (fair or unfair treatment based on language characteristics by a person or group) or institutional (practices or policies that exclude, limit or disadvantage someone based on language.) Prejudice can also be based on one's language proficiency or ability to speak in an "official," "national" or "approved" language. In the US, there have been many attempts to make English the official national language of the country. While there are many prejudicial and partisan reasons for favoring English, opponents believe any official language would violate the linguistic rights and diversity of the nation's population, would make no positive contribution to national unity and communication, and would be detrimental to global competitiveness and US diplomacy.

Accentism, which is prejudice based on one's accent or enunciation, is common around the world and introduces indelible stereotypes and stigmas into human interactions. An example of stereotyping in the US is judging people who speak with a southern accent as less intelligent, less educated, less competent or more conservative than those who do not have a southern accent. People in the UK who speak cockney may be stereotyped as coming from a lower class than those who use standard British English, or as being untrustworthy, possibly even criminal. The corollary is that in the US, people who speak with the more precise diction of standard British English may be stereotyped as having higher intelligence, higher education and greater trustworthiness than those who speak standard American English. Stigmatizing, which is the process of devaluing or marginalizing someone based on accent, often results in social exclusivism, shame and low self-esteem. A southern accent may target someone for mockery or ridicule and lower the prospects for employment or job advancement.

Prejudice based on language, like all prejudices, demonstrates society's propensity to divide itself into smaller and smaller groups of like individuals for the purpose of elevating one's own groups and devaluing the others, usually for some advantage. The disunity caused by these divisions is a chief cause of disharmony in the world.

The communication difficulties of multiple languages and dialects was dramatized in the Old Testament in the origin myth of the Tower of Babel.[128] In this colorful tale, the people of Shinar (Babylonia), who had grown disobedient and ambitious, attempted to build a magnificent tower that would reach all the way to heaven. As punishment for their pride and the folly of human self-sufficiency, God confused their speech and scattered the people throughout the world, explaining the diversity of human languages and indicating that God knew the problems this would cause.

The many difficulties created by multiple languages have been addressed by the world's latest wisdom tradition, which provides guidance for dealing with many contemporary issues previously unaddressed by religion. This new wisdom tradition promotes the principle of an international auxiliary language.

> A universal language would make intercourse possible with every nation. Thus it would be needful to know two languages only, the mother tongue and the universal speech. The latter would enable a man to communicate with any and every man in the world! A third language would not be needed. To be able to talk with a member of any race and country without requiring an interpreter, how helpful and restful to all![129]

Certainly, the ultimate achievement of universal peace would require such an auxiliary language and it is impossible to imagine any drawbacks.

---

128 *The Bible*, Genesis 11:1-9.
129 'Abdu'l-Bahá, *Paris Talks*, p. 156.

> Oneness of language will transform mankind into one world, remove religious misunderstandings, and unite East and West in the spirit of brotherhood and love. Oneness of language will change this world from many families into one family. This auxiliary international language will gather the nations under one standard, as if the five continents of the world had become one, for then mutual interchange of thought will be possible for all. It will remove ignorance and superstition, since each child of whatever race or nation can pursue his studies in science and art, needing but two languages -- his own and the International... Then the nations will be enabled to utilize the latest and best thought...[130]

Prejudice against Women

The need to eliminate prejudice against women and at last establish the equality of women and men has never been more acute. After decades of significant gains in women's rights and stature in many countries, a sudden erosion of previous momentum has occurred. This topic is of such urgency and importance that we have dedicated an entire chapter to the topic.

---

130 'Abdu'l-Bahá, *Bahá'í Scriptures*, p. 339.

Chapter 7:
Equality of Women and Men

Eve's Fault

Prejudice is opportunistic. It may lay dormant for a time, but when an opportunity appears, it cannot help but show itself. Such an opportunity arose early in the Old Testament. The second chapter of Genesis tells the vivid origin myth of the creation of Adam and Eve. It certainly was not documented history because only the starring characters were there to write it down. Yet based on this short and fantastic tale, and similar ones in other traditions, the plight of women has been sadly suppressed for millennia. Throughout the ages, the priests and other interpreters of scriptures—mostly males, of course, and likely biased in favor of their gender—found ample opportunity in that ancient parable to justify their innate selfish prejudice. Or so it seems.

According to the biblical narrative, Adam was created first, establishing for many the supremacy of the male gender. This notion appears to be supported by the method of Eve's creation from one of Adam's ribs. According to Genesis 2:21–24, God created Eve out of Adam's source material, making her a second-generation human.

> And the LORD God caused a deep sleep to fall upon Adam, and he slept: and he took one of his ribs, and closed up the flesh instead thereof; and the rib, which the LORD God had taken from man, made he a woman, and brought her unto the man. And Adam said, This is now bone of my bones, and flesh of my flesh: she shall be called Woman, because she was taken out of Man.[131]

In addition, we learn that God's intention was to make Eve a suitable sexual partner for Adam; after all, only a female can give birth and propagate the new world with offspring. It is understandable that many commentators on this story inferred that Eve was weaker and of second-class status to Adam.

The origin story describes how a talking serpent then tempted Eve to eat from the tree of the knowledge of good and evil, the fruit of which God had forbidden them to eat or touch.

> And when the woman saw that the tree was good for food, and that it was pleasant to the eyes, and a tree to be desired to make one wise, she took of the fruit thereof, and did eat, and gave also unto her husband with her; and he did eat.[132]

The author of the tale, perhaps to avoid the inevitable immorality issue of fornication to be revealed later, turned Adam into Eve's "husband." God cursed the serpent to crawl on its belly forevermore. For Eve's disobedience, God sentenced her to endure childbearing.

> Unto the woman he said, I will greatly multiply thy sorrow and thy conception; in sorrow thou shalt bring forth children.[133]

---

131 *The Bible*, Genesis 2:21-24
132 *The Bible*, Genesis 3:7
133 *The Bible*, Genesis 3:16.

Also, in the following words, the author has God set an indelible precedent for theologians to claim the inferiority of women to men:

> ...thy desire shall be to thy husband, and he shall rule over thee.[134]

Thus, the fate of women was sealed for thousands of years and the tyranny against them remained unchecked. Later interpreters apparently were so impressed with evidence of female preeminence in sinfulness that they brushed over an earlier passage in Genesis:

> And God said, Let us make man in our image, after our likeness.[135]

This verse highlights the equal worth and value of both men and women by stating that both genders are created in the image of God, thus neither could be inferior or subservient to the other. The newest wisdom tradition confirms that this verse refers to both genders:

> Man is a generic term applying to all humanity.... The image and likeness of God apply to her [Eve] as well.... to accept and observe a distinction which God has not intended in creation is ignorance and superstition.[136]

Elsewhere, a passage provides a rational explanation of the symbology of the story of Adam and Eve. In biblical passages, we are told, the name Adam refers symbolically to the first Divine Educator of humanity, the first Manifestation of God, whose name has been lost. This account also clarifies that the story was not a factual retelling of an historical event but rather symbolic in nature.

---

134 *The Bible*, Genesis 3:16.
135 *The Bible*, Genesis 1:26.
136 'Abdu'l-Bahá, *The Promulgation of Universal Peace*.

> If the outward meaning of this account were to be attributed to a wise man, all men of wisdom would assuredly deny it, arguing that such a scheme and arrangement could not possibly have proceeded from such a person. The account of Adam and Eve, their eating from the tree, and their expulsion from Paradise are therefore symbols and divine mysteries... These verses of the Torah have therefore numerous meanings.[137]

No one can confirm who authored the book of Genesis and other books in the Pentateuch, though they are all credited to Moses. Most modern scholars place the authorship of these books in the sixth to fifth centuries BC, hundreds of years after Moses's time. There are certain "postmosaica" passages in the Pentateuch that describe events that occurred after Moses's death. Other "amosaica" verses, such as Numbers 12:4, include a sudden shift to a third-person point-of-view that would be awkward for Moses to have written: "Suddenly the Lord said to Moses and Aaron and to Miriam, "You three come out to the tent of meeting..."

If some of these passages were added later to Moses's tablets, we are left not knowing what Moses wrote and didn't write. We are also left with the suspicion that Moses may not have written any of these books.

The issue of authorship of Genesis or the extent of text editing becomes important when we consider the paradox between the claim of equality of women and men in Genesis 1:26-27 and the sudden shift to women's subjugation by men as a punishment. Such penalties are claimed by evangelicals and others to illustrate the price that Eve and all subsequent women paid because of Eve's disobedience. At one time, say proponents of this view, Eve had equal status with Adam, but this status was removed because of her sin, and the penalty remains in force today. It is possible that this rebalancing

---

137 'Abdu'l-Bahá, *Some Answered Questions*.

of Eve's status was inserted later into the origin story as a pretext to justify a common sixth-century BC view of women's inferior status.

Other Creation Myths

Jews, Christians and Muslims are most familiar with the Adam and Eve creation story, but there are many variations around the world that have common elements—the loneliness of the first man; a woman created to be the man's companion; the woman eventually initiating a separation from the creator; the man and woman becoming the parents of the human race.

Originally, all these stories were passed down orally and revised as they were remembered and retold thousands of times. Also, the stories are thought to be true by some in the native cultures but thought of as myths by most others. These creation stories illustrate the rich imagination of humans to reach for an understanding of how things began, but also demonstrate that we should not take the specifics too literally. If earlier stages of civilization would have appreciated the story of Adam and Eve as a parable about obedience to God's will instead of focusing on the fictional details, women may have avoided an abundance of suffering.

There are numerous ancient stories featuring main characters like Adam and Eve. The details of these stories do not perfectly match up, of course, but historical accuracy is not the point of myths. The stories are generally referred to as: The Greek Apocalypse of Moses; the Latin Life of Adam and Eve; the Armenian Penitence of Adam; the Georgian Book of Adam. There are also some fragmentary Coptic versions of stories. These various writings include fanciful adventures of Adam and Eve after their expulsion from the Garden of Eden, details about the Fall of Man, and the story of Satan's fall from grace from Eve's point of view.

Here are ten other creation stories from around the world that you can find on the Internet. It is beyond the scope of this book to summarize each of them.

1. Agikuyu creation story from the largest tribe in Kenya.
2. Bald Eagle creation story from the Salinan Indians in the US.
3. Bukusu creation story from the Bantu in Kenya.
4. Biami creation story from Papua New Guinea.
5. Blackfeet Indian creation story from the US.
6. Fang creation story from West Africa.
7. Norse creation story from Norway.
8. Efik and the Meal in Heaven creation story from Nigeria.
9. Eridu Genesis creation story from Sumeria.
10. Indian creation story from the Hindu Upanishads.

Religious Contributions to Prejudice against Women

For thousands of years, most likely, deep-seated prejudice against women has even polluted texts considered authoritative and religious. No wonder the world has felt justified treating women like second class citizens—or worse. At around 500 BC, Confucius betrayed his reputation for wisdom by writing:

> Such is the stupidity of women's character that it is incumbent upon her, in every particular, to distrust herself and to obey her husband.[138]

A couple of hundred years later, the following advice appeared in a Hindu text named in honor of the semi-legendary "first man" Manu:

> In childhood a woman must be subject to her father; in youth, to her husband; when her husband is dead, to her sons. A woman must never be free of subjugation.[139]

---

138 Confucius, Confucian Marriage Manual.
139 *The Hindu Code of Manu*, dated about 250 BC, which regulates social

> If a wife has no children after eight years of marriage, she shall be banished; if all of her children are dead, she can be dismissed after ten years; and, if she produces only girls she shall be repudiated after eleven years.[140]

New Testament Contributions to Prejudice against Women

It should not be surprising that male views about the role and rights of women would work their way into Christian Scriptures. Men authored these works, and biases have a nasty tendency to influence reporting and interpretation of human affairs. In the New Testament, we can find cringeworthy advice like the following:

> Wives, submit yourselves to your own husbands as you do to the Lord. For the husband is the head of the wife as Christ is the head of the church, his body, of which he is the Savior. Now as the church submits to Christ, so also wives should submit to their husbands in everything.[141]

> A woman should learn in quietness and full submission. I do not permit a woman to teach or to assume authority over a man; she must be quiet.[142]

> . . . women should be silent in the churches. For they are not permitted to speak, but should be subordinate,

---

customs and provides detailed precepts for daily life.
   140 *The Hindu Code of Manu*, dated about 250 BC, which regulates social customs and provides detailed precepts for daily life.
   141 *The Bible*, Ephesians 5:22-24.
   142 *The Bible*, 1 Timothy 2:11-12.

> as the law also says. If there is anything they desire to know, let them ask their husbands at home. For it is shameful for a woman to speak in church.[143]

> Every man who prays or prophesies with his head covered dishonors his head. But every woman who prays or prophesies with her head uncovered dishonors her head—it is the same as having her head shaved. For if a woman does not cover her head, she might as well have her hair cut off.[144]

In the Quran, the concept of modesty is emphasized for everyone, but greater restraint is required of women. In some societies, penalties for disobedience can involve shaming, beatings and even death:

> And tell the believing women to reduce [some] of their vision and guard their private parts and not expose their adornment except that which [necessarily] appears thereof and to wrap [a portion of] their headcovers over their chests.[145]

Verses like these—often misquoted, misunderstood or taken out of context—have been used as weapons of manipulation for those who seek justification for restricting women's rights. These passages are brandished like whips to justify restrictive dress codes for women; rejection of women priests, pastors or mullas; and total wifely subservience to husbands, even abusive ones. Some biblical scholars see reflected in these New Testament scriptures the apparently sexist views of the author, St. Paul, or possibly disciples writing on his behalf.

---

143 *The Bible*, 1 Corinthians 14:34-35.
144 *The Bible*, 1 Corinthians 11:4-6
145 *Quran*, Verse 24:31.

To Paul's credit, he also wrote a letter to Jewish Christians in the southern region of the Roman province of Galatia in which he obliquely mentioned the equality of women and men.

> There is neither Jew nor Greek, there is neither bond nor free, there is neither male nor female; for ye are all one in Christ Jesus.[146]

Members of the south Galatian churches were warring among themselves about the need to continue following the old Jewish laws, such as male circumcision, and Paul harshly criticized these false beliefs by stressing the need to become "one in Christ Jesus." It is impossible to know if using the words "there is neither male nor female" was his way of stating a spiritual principle of equality or merely a literary flourish to emphasize his main theme.

Some Christian theologians have defended Paul's contradictions as the result of translating or copying errors, or possibly later insertions or corrections. Whether the impact of these passages was intentional or inadvertent, Paul's words have been used to reduce women's freedoms and opportunities for centuries. As we will see, the world's wisdom traditions provide ample support for the equality of women and men.

Wisdom Traditions Favor Women's Equality

It is unfortunate that a handful of passages from the world's wisdom traditions have misled individuals or were hijacked to deliver a message of the necessity of women's inequality with men. The opposite is true.

Like most religions, Judaism has had a complex relationship with the topic of gender equality, and the religion's various sects have different perspectives. Issues like women's access to religious leadership positions, women's participation in some rituals and the interpretation of Jewish law continue to be discussed and debated.

---

146 *The Bible*, Galatians 3:28.

Nevertheless, in the Old Testament, numerous women play significant roles and make major contributions to their societies. In the Book of Judges, Deborah is both a prophet and a judge. She led the Israelites in battle and delivered wise guidance to her people, showing that it was acceptable in Judaism for a woman to be a military leader and an arbiter of justice.[147] Other esteemed and influential women in the Old Testament were Esther and Ruth, whose individual exceptionality does not diminish their status as equal to men in their societies.

In the New Testament, Jesus emphasized the equality of women and men. He always treated women with respect and dignity and often had meaningful conversations with them, which broke with current social norms. He lovingly valued their contributions and acknowledged their faith. Good examples include the conversation he had with the Samaritan woman at the well[148] and his praise for the faith of the woman who anointed his feet.[149] Actions sometimes express spiritual principles better than words.

The Quran also teaches the equal worth and value of men and women.

> Indeed, the Muslim men and Muslim women, the believing men and believing women, the obedient men and obedient women, the truthful men and truthful women, the patient men and patient women, the humble men and humble women, the charitable men and charitable women, the fasting men and fasting women, the men who guard their private parts and the women who do so—for them, Allah has prepared forgiveness and a great reward.[150]

---

147 *The Bible*, Judges 4-5.
148 *The Bible*, John 4.
149 *The Bible*, Luke 7:36-50.
150 *Quran*, Verse 33:35.

The passage above establishes that piety and righteousness are not gender-specific and both men and women are equally rewarded for their good deeds. The Quran also acknowledges the essential roles that women play in society and grants women the right to own and inherit property and actively participate in economic affairs.

> And do not wish for that by which Allah has made some of you exceed others. For men is a share of what they have earned, and for women is a share of what they have earned. And ask Allah of His bounty. Indeed, Allah is ever, of all things, Knowing.[151]

This verse emphasizes the equal right of both men and women to enjoy the fruits of their labor and be treated with justice in matters of property and finance. Like Jesus, the Prophet Muhammad set an example of treating women with kindness, respect and equality. He strongly advocated for women in marriage, inheritance and decision-making. He often consulted respectfully with his wives and female acquaintances in a spirit of partnership. Despite these original teachings, numerous traditions and extremist elements have sharpened the edges of female suppression and brutally punished imaginary offenses against Islamic law.

Understanding and Fostering Equality of the Sexes

Human civilization is constantly evolving and its collective intellect is ever-advancing through more inclusiveness in religious sensemaking. This evolution is represented by an exploding number of scientific discoveries, broader educational opportunities for more people, and innovations in communications technology that foster an ever-widening perspective on human rights. Religion ought to be a major contributor to resolving emerging issues of the age like climate change as well as old issues to which society has recently awakened and

---

151 *Quran*, Verse 4:32

declared relevant to everyone on earth, such as equality of the sexes. In a statement from our most recent wisdom tradition, we learn that:

> The rational soul does not merely occupy a private sphere, but is an active participant in a social order. Although the received truths of the great faiths remain valid, the daily experience of an individual in the twenty-first century is unimaginably removed from the one that he or she would have known in any of those ages when this guidance was revealed. Democratic decision-making has fundamentally altered the relationship of the individual to authority. With growing confidence and growing success, women justly insist on their right to full equality with men.[152]

The dynamics of human will are vividly manifest at the collective level in recent mass social movements, notably the women's movement, the civil rights movement, the antinuclear movement and the Indigenous People's movement. All of these have involved a wide range of activities, but studies about these movements have primarily focused on political conflict and ignored the spiritual component.

The roots of the women's movement, often referred to as feminism, stretch back to the Enlightenment period of the eighteenth century when early activists and feminist thinkers such as Mary Wollstonecraft began advocating for women's education and civil rights. Certainly, throughout history, individual women have stood up for their rights, but Wollstonecraft and her compatriots represent the first collective struggle for gender equality, social justice and the recognition of women's rights around the globe.

Historians tend to mark a pivotal moment in 1848 as the true beginning of the women's movement. That year, at the Seneca Falls Convention in the Finger Lakes District of New York, suffragettes including Susan B. Anthony and Elizabeth Cady Stanton drafted a

---

152 The Universal House of Justice, *One Common Faith*.

Declaration of Sentiments demanding women's right to vote and equality under the law.

That same year, in the Persian hamlet of Badasht, a brilliant and highly educated woman named Ṭáhirih, who was raised in the center of traditional Islamic culture, dared to appear unveiled at a gathering of followers of our most recent wisdom tradition.

> **Her unruffled serenity sharply contrasted with the affrighted countenances of those who were gazing upon her face. Fear, anger, and bewilderment stirred the depths of their souls. That sudden revelation seemed to have stunned their faculties.**[153]

Her meaning was undoubtedly understood by many as a proclamation of the advent of a New Day that would transcend cultural constraints and would bring about a revolutionary transformation in human society.

Her uncovering was so dramatic that some of her co-believers, who had grown up in Islam, had difficulty accepting that a woman would appear publicly unveiled and speaking directly to men. These are the words she spoke: "The Trumpet is sounding! The Great Trump is blown! The universal Advent is now proclaimed!"[154] Ṭáhirih was martyred in 1852.

This historical display by a woman caught the attention of observers, as did her life and martyrdom. Leading European orientalists, such as E.G. Browne, Carl Friedrich Andreas and Theodor Nöldeke, analyzed Tahirih's life and texts. European artists and novelists, such as Marie von Najmajer, Isabella Grinevskaya and Sarah Bernhardt, paid tribute to the life of the Persian poet and martyr. Certainly, Tahirih's courageous act gave urgency and legitimacy to the subject of women's rights globally.

---

153 Nabil, *The Dawn-Breakers*.
154 'Abdu'l-Bahá, *Memorials of the Faithful*.

In truth, the 1848 Seneca Falls Convention was held four years after the emergence of our most recent wisdom tradition in Persia, today called the Bahá'í Faith, which directly challenged many long-held beliefs including the inferiority of women and their obligatory submission to male authority. It is from these Teachings that Táhirih gained her courage and boldness. The threat of these new teachings to clerical power and male domination set off a firestorm of brutal persecution that slaughtered hundreds of thousands and, perhaps, released into the world a spiritual impulse by so boldly shattering outdated traditions.

The brutality of the repression underscored how deeply the current religious leaders feared the power of these new Teachings to destroy the old principles by which they maintained near-absolute dominance over half their population. With respect to the advancement of women, the new wisdom tradition affirmed:

- *Spiritual equality.* A central tenet of the new wisdom tradition was that both genders possessed equal capacities for spiritual advancement, and so women should have the same opportunities as men to seek knowledge and engage in religious devotion.
- *Educational equality.* The new "heresy," as it was called, encouraged female education, a radical departure from prevailing nineteenth century social norms in Persia. The new Teachings clearly stated that women had a fundamental right to go to school and acquire knowledge so they could be full participants in religious and societal affairs.
- *Women as spiritual leaders.* In teaching a new path by example, the new wisdom tradition included Tahirih, a woman, in a group of eighteen called the Letters of the Living. This group, comparable to Jesus's twelve disciples, played a significant role in spreading the Teach-

ings. Tahirih became a prominent figure in the growing community.

These principles have had a transformative effect on women's status in Persia and beyond, laying the foundation for a movement that continues striving for gender equality and social justice for women.

Arguments against the Women's Movement

In the US, the women's movement for equality and social justice has been largely a political endeavor. Gender equality has inevitably become the cause of disunity based on numerous criticisms from different perspectives including diverse political ideologies, social values and religious beliefs. The most common political criticisms leveled at the "women's movement" in general include these:

1. *Opposition to traditional gender roles.* Critics often say that efforts to achieve gender equality undermine traditional gender roles that are vital for the stability of society and family structures. The result, they fear, can disrupt society and destroy traditional family values.
2. *Cultural relativism.* Critics from culturally conservative backgrounds argue that the movement for gender equality, which was born in a Western context, attempts to graft Western values and feminist ideals onto cultures and societies that have different values and traditions.
3. *Inappropriate focus on identity politics.* Some critics worry that the women's movement, particularly as it has been interwoven with identity politics, excessively focuses on specific identities (race, ethnicity, sexual orientations, et cetera). They worry that this can have the unintended consequence of increasing conflict and division rather than helping to create a more unified approach to gender equality.

4. *Radicalization of feminism and misandry.* Some radical feminist factions have provoked criticism for misandry—the hatred of or hostility toward men. These critics, who seek to promote gender equality, believe such radicalization goes too far, alienating potential allies perpetuating gender-based animosity instead of promoting cooperation between genders.
5. *Negative impact on family and marriage.* Some critics contend that advocacy for women's rights and opportunities in the workplace may have contributed to negative changes in traditional family structures, leading to a decline in marriages, an increase in the divorce rate and an accompanying deterioration of children's wellbeing.
6. *Misguided focus on victimhood.* A common criticism in some instances is that emphasizing gender equality portrays women as unceasing victims of patriarchy, a perspective that may undermine women's agency and empowerment by promoting a narrative of helplessness.
1. *Exclusion of men.* Some critics claim that the women's movement sometimes reinforces gender-based divisions and dismisses or marginalizes men's perspectives and issues, which can limit male alliances.

The women's movement, of course, is not a monolithic entity, so criticisms vary significantly depending on which specific group or faction is asked. Regrettably, many of the criticisms are of specific political factions supporting gender equality, not of the concept of equality itself. The criticisms we summarized show the handicap of looking for a political solution to what many individuals now see as a spiritual problem—one of the heart as well as the mind. By politicizing this important issue, sides inevitably are defined, and people of both genders may feel required to take sides, which can create even more disunity.

Advancing the Status of Women

In the view of the world's most recent wisdom tradition, the creation of an ever-advancing society leading to a peaceful and sustainable world civilization is impossible without women fully participating in every arena of human activity.

> When all mankind shall receive the same opportunity of education and the equality of men and women be realized, the foundations of war will be utterly destroyed. Without equality this will be impossible because all differences and distinction are conducive to discord and strife. Equality between men and women is conducive to the abolition of warfare for the reason that women will never be willing to sanction it. Mothers will not give their sons as sacrifices upon the battlefield after twenty years of anxiety and loving devotion in rearing them from infancy, no matter what cause they are called upon to defend. There is no doubt that when women obtain equality of rights, war will entirely cease among mankind.[155]

While many individuals support gender equality, there is a great difference between intellectual support and heartfelt submission to it as an essential human value at last clarified by the following passage:

> Let it be known once more that until woman and man recognize and realize equality, social and political progress here or anywhere will not be possible. For the world of humanity consists of two parts or members: one is woman; the other is man. Until these two members are equal in strength, the oneness of humanity cannot be established, and the happiness and felicity of mankind will not be a reality.[156]

---

155 'Abdu'l-Bahá, *The Promulgation of Universal Peace*, pp.174–175.
156 'Abdu'l-Bahá, *The Promulgation of Universal Peace*, p.77.

In the past, it has been mainly women who have fought to achieve gender equality. This is understandable as males have enjoyed the comforts and perks of domination since the appearance of humans on the planet. But for gender equality to become universally accepted will require men to join the mission.

> It is time for the institutions of the world, composed mainly of men, to use their influence to promote the systematic inclusion of women, not out of condescension or presumed self-sacrifice but as an act motivated by the belief that the contributions of women are required for society to progress.[157]

In the following words, the latest wisdom tradition provided much-needed hope for the achievement of greater gender equality accomplished by the dedicated efforts of dedicated individuals following a clear plan of action:

> The world in the past has been ruled by force, and man has dominated over woman by reason of his more forceful and aggressive qualities both of body and mind. But the balance is already shifting—force is losing its weight and mental alertness, intuition, and the spiritual qualities of love and service, in which woman is strong, are gaining ascendancy. Hence the new age will be an age less masculine, and more permeated with the feminine ideals—or, to speak more exactly, will be an age in which the masculine and feminine elements of civilization will be more evenly balanced.[158]

---

157 "A Turning Point for All Nations," a statement prepared by the Bahá'í International Community United Nations Office, New York.

158 'Abdu'lBahá, quoted in John E. Esslemont, *Bahá'u'lláh and the New Era*, p. 156.

According to a whitepaper by the Bahá'í International Community United Nations Office, these are the urgent points of emphasis for achieving this promised future:

Violence against Women

> First and foremost, violence against women and girls, one of the most blatant and widespread abuses of human rights, must be eradicated. Violence has been a fact of life for many women throughout the world, regardless of race, class, or educational background. In many societies, traditional beliefs that women are inferior or a burden make them easy targets of anger and frustration. Even strong legal remedies and enforcement mechanisms will have little effect until they are supported by a transformation in the attitudes of men. Women will not be safe until a new social conscience takes hold, one which will make the mere expression of condescending attitudes towards women, let alone any form of physical violence, a cause for deep shame.[159]

Everywhere in our world, women face violence in many forms and degrees. According to the World Health Organization (WHO), about one-third of women worldwide has experienced physical and/or sexual violence in their lifetimes. This statistic may be underestimated since many incidents of violence go unreported due to fear, stigma and cultural barriers.

A distressing aspect of this crisis is the high prevalence of intimate partner violence (IPV). Women are disproportionately affected by violence at the hands of their current or former partners. IPV can lead to physical injuries, emotional trauma and death. In

---

159 "A Turning Point for All Nations," a statement prepared by the Bahá'í International Community United Nations Office, New York.

some regions, dowry-related violence and "honor killings" illustrate the extreme forms of violence that women endure.

Sexual violence is another deeply concerning aspect. Widespread rape, sexual assault and harassment are issues that affect women of all ages with devastating and long-term consequences. In areas of political or military conflict, sexual violence is frequently used as a weapon of war, targeting women to terrorize and displace communities.

Violence against women overlaps with other forms of discrimination. Women from minority ethnic, racial, and religious groups and those with disabilities or from low-income backgrounds are particularly vulnerable. The combining of these identities compounds the risks and barriers faced in seeking help and protection against violence.

Focus on the Family

> **Second, the family remains the basic building block of society and behaviors observed and learned there will be projected onto interactions at all other levels of society. Therefore, the members of the institution of the family must be transformed so that the principle of equality of women and men is internalized. Further, if the bonds of love and unity cement family relationships, the impact will reach beyond its borders and affect society as a whole.**[160]

The recent crisis in the disintegration of family units is often caused by rapid urbanization, globalization and economic shifts. The migration of more individuals to urban centers for better opportunities often leads to the fragmentation of traditional families. Divorce rates have risen greatly in many parts of the globe because of changing societal norms and shifting personal priorities. Economic hardships and

---

160 "A Turning Point for All Nations," a statement prepared by the Bahá'í International Community United Nations Office, New York.

unemployment can lead to relationship conflicts and family break-ups. The rise of single-parent households caused by unplanned pregnancies, spousal deaths and divorces contribute to the dilemma, as does substance abuse, addiction and mental health challenges.

The rise of gender equality and greater financial independence for women is often blamed as a significant factor in family break-ups, but when combined with love, respect and appreciation of each spouse for the other, the embracing of gender equality can eliminate conflicts and help teach all family members this important human value so future generations will appreciate its virtues.

Education of Women and Girls

> Third, while the overall goal of any society must be to educate all its members, at this stage in human history the greatest need is to educate women and girls. For over twenty years, studies have consistently documented that, of all possible investments, educating women and girls pays the highest overall dividends in terms of social development, the eradication of poverty and the advancement of community.[161],[162]

That women and girls should receive priority over men and boys in access to education has been a long-standing principle in the Teachings of our most recent wisdom tradition, which back in 1912 proclaimed:

> ...that men and women are equal in the sight of God and that there is no distinction to be made between

---

161 Lawrence H. Summers, Vice President & Chief Economist for the World Bank, Investing in All the People. 1992. Also, USAID. 1989. Technical Reports in Gender and Development. Making the Case for the Gender Variable: Women and the Wealth and Well-being of Nations. Office of Women in Development.

162 "A Turning Point for All Nations," a statement prepared by the Bahá'í International Community United Nations Office, New York.

> them. The only difference between them now is due to lack of education and training. If woman is given equal opportunity of education, distinction and estimate of inferiority will disappear.... Furthermore, the education of women is of greater importance than the education of men, for they are the mothers of the race, and mothers rear the children. The first teachers of children are the mothers. Therefore, they must be capably trained in order to educate both sons and daughters. There are many provisions in... regard to this. He [Bahá'u'lláh] promulgated the adoption of the same course of education for man and woman. Daughters and sons must follow the same curriculum of study, thereby promoting unity of the sexes."[163]

Gender Complementarity

> ...the global dialogue on the role of men and women must promote recognition of the intrinsic complementarity of the two sexes. For the differences between them are a natural assertion of the necessity of women and men to work together to bring to fruition their potentialities for advancing civilization, no less than for perpetuating the human race. Such differences are inherent in the interactive character of their common humanity. This dialogue needs to consider the historical forces which have led to the oppression of women and examine the new social, political and spiritual realities which are today transforming our civilization.[164]

If a woman's role as mother is correctly valued, her work in nurturing

---

163 'Abdu'lBahá, *The Promulgation of Universal Peace*, pp.174–175.
164 "A Turning Point for All Nations," a statement prepared by the Bahá'í International Community United Nations Office, New York.

and educating children will be respected and properly rewarded. Her child-bearing role does not diminish one's aptitude for leadership or diminish her intellectual, scientific or creative capacities. In fact, it may enhance those abilities. The necessary biological gender differences should not be a cause for inequality or disunity. Rather, they can be viewed as complementary.

> **Humanity is like a bird with its two wings—the one is male, the other female. Unless both wings are strong and impelled by some common force, the bird cannot fly heavenwards. According to the spirit of this age, women must advance and fulfill their mission in all departments of life, becoming equal to men. They must be on the same level as men and enjoy equal rights.**[165]

True and lasting progress toward acceptance of gender equality cannot be won through violent confrontations, power struggles, or political action, but only through self-evaluation and a process of spiritual evolution that transforms the basic values by which we live and interact. Personal accountability and incremental change are the fundamental processes that produce advanced and enduring civilizations, for they ensure the ability to adapt and survive in changing conditions and circumstances.

---

165 Cited to 'Abdu'l-Bahá in *Bahá'u'lláh and the New Era*.

Chapter 8:
Universal Education

Revealing Treasures

According to the United Nations Educational, Scientific and Cultural Organization (UNESCO), education is a basic human right that lifts men and women out of poverty, cures inequalities, provides growth opportunities and is the most sustainable investment available. Yet today, nearly a quarter billion children and youth are out of school because of social, cultural or economic reasons. Nearly a hundred million of them are in Sub-Saharan Africa. Only 70 percent of the world's countries legally guarantee at least nine years of compulsory education. Nearly three-quarters of a billion young people and adults lack basic literacy skills; two-thirds of these are women.[166]

In the US, which has the highest disposable income per capita in the world, nearly one out of five adults are illiterate. Over half read or write below a sixth-grade level. It's literacy rate ranks 125th among all countries, below Oman, Burundi and Botswana.[167] About 52 percent of American children don't go to school.[168]

---

166 https://www.unesco.org/en/right-education/
167 https://www.crossrivertherapy.com/research/literacy-statistics#literacy-rate-by-gender.
168 https://datacenter.aecf.org/data/tables/9010-young-children-not-in-school

For those who prize the human potential of each individual—and not all do—education is the essential ingredient in achieving an ever-advancing civilization.

> Regard man as a mine rich in gems of inestimable value. Education can, alone, cause it to reveal its treasures, and enable mankind to benefit therefrom.[169]

In all aspects of life—whether one learns through private study, is formally taught in schools or accumulates knowledge from nature and experience—education is the remedy for one of the most devastating illnesses of our planet.

> The primary, the most urgent requirement is the promotion of education. It is inconceivable that any nation should achieve prosperity and success unless this paramount, this fundamental concern is carried forward. The principal reason for the decline and fall of peoples is ignorance. Today the mass of the people are uninformed even as to ordinary affairs, how much less do they grasp the core of the important problems and complex needs of the time.[170]

The latest wisdom tradition stresses that because ignorance and a lack of education are barriers of separation among humankind…

> …all must receive training and instruction. Through this provision the lack of mutual understanding will be remedied and the unity of mankind furthered and advanced. Universal education is a universal law.[171]

---

169 Bahá'u'lláh, *Tablets of Bahá'u'lláh*, Lawh-i-Maqsúd
170 'Abdu'l-Bahá, *The Secret of Divine Civilization*.
171 'Abdu'l-Bahá, *The Promulgation of World Peace*.

By "universal law," the authors understand the meaning of this statement to be that universal education is a spiritual truth, a human right. This statement was made about a century before UNESCO declared education a human right.

Compulsory Education

Among the core tenets of this new wisdom tradition is the fundamental principle of compulsory education for everyone. Rationally, this is a hard point to dispute, though there are practical reasons why the world has not pursued this more vigorously—short-sighted debates about social priorities, economic feasibility, religious biases, cultural norms, et cetera.

Regarding social priorities, we have been told that education is "the most urgent requirement" we have to unify and advance our society. The economic feasibility issue evaporates when we understand that education may be our greatest sustainable investment, paying dividends for each individual with expanded opportunities and society as a whole with greater productivity and innovation. Religious biases against education for women and girls are frankly relics of a past age that diminish human dignity and the advancement of civilization. Cultural norms are merely traditions—ghosts of ancient practices that will disappear just as superstitions do with time and knowledge.

> It is for this reason that, in this new cycle, education and training are recorded in the Book of God as obligatory and not voluntary. That is, it is enjoined upon the father and mother, as a duty, to strive with all effort to train the daughter and the son, to nurse them from the breast of knowledge and to rear them in the bosom of sciences and arts. Should they neglect this matter, they shall be held responsible and worthy of reproach in the presence of the stern Lord.[172]

---

172 'Abdu'l-Bahá, *Selections from the Writings of 'Abdu'l-Bahá*.

In this age, responsibility for guaranteeing the education of children is clearly placed on the parents. Education is the sacred duty of each mother and father. Many kinds of hardships can interfere with this responsibility, but throughout the world we find examples of parents joining forces to educate their children when schools are not available.

> The education of each child is compulsory. In addition to this wide-spread education each child must be taught a profession, art, or trade, so that every member of the community will be enabled to earn his own livelihood. Work done in the spirit of service is the highest form of worship.[173]

Importance of the Family

According to the guidance of the new wisdom tradition, the family is considered a sacred institution and a cohesive collection of souls who share not only a bloodline but also learning experiences. Every member of a family is both a teacher and a student. The acquisition of human virtues, which is the primary goal, is a shared experience because neither the parents nor the children are perfectly virtuous. The sanctity and unity of the family, which is the primary classroom for the spiritual and moral education of parents and their children, must be preserved at all costs if we are to bring about an ever-advancing civilization. This explains the need for guidance such as this:

> According to the teachings of Bahá'u'lláh [Prophet-Founder of the latest wisdom tradition] the family, being a human unit, must be educated according to the rules of sanctity. All the virtues must be taught

---

173 'Abdu'l-Bahá, *Compilation on Women,* available at https://www.bahai.org/library/authoritative-texts/compilations/women/3#329616910, #47.

> the family. The integrity of the family bond must be constantly considered, and the rights of the individual members must not be transgressed. The rights of the son, the father, the mother—none of them must be transgressed, none of them must be arbitrary. Just as the son has certain obligations to his father, the father, likewise, has certain obligations to his son. The mother, the sister and other members of the household have their certain prerogatives. All these rights and prerogatives must be conserved, yet the unity of the family must be sustained. The injury of one shall be considered the injury of all; the comfort of each, the comfort of all; the honor of one, the honor of all.[174]

Children are every family's and nation's most prized possession because they are the future.

> Children are the most precious treasure a community can possess, for in them are the promise and guarantee of the future. They bear the seeds of the character of future society which is largely shaped by what the adults constituting the community do or fail to do with respect to children. They are a trust no community can neglect with impunity. An all-embracing love of children, the manner of treating them, the quality of the attention shown them, the spirit of adult behavior toward them—these are all among the vital aspects of the requisite attitude. Love demands discipline, the courage to accustom children to hardship, not to indulge their whims or leave them entirely to their own devices. An atmosphere needs to be maintained in which children feel that they belong to the community and share in its purpose…[175]

---

174 'Abdu'l-Bahá, *The Promulgation of World Peace*.
175 The Universal House of Justice, "To the Bahá'ís of the World," Ridván

Young children are most easily taught human virtues As they get older, they often become more set in their ways and resistant to parental advice guidance.

> It is extremely difficult to teach the individual and refine his character once puberty is passed. By then, as experience hath shown, even if every effort be exerted to modify some tendency of his, it all availeth nothing. He may, perhaps, improve somewhat today; but let a few days pass and he forgetteth, and turneth backward to his habitual condition and accustomed ways. Therefore it is in early childhood that a firm foundation must be laid. While the branch is green and tender it can easily be made straight.[176]

In too many cases, however, parents and other adults who are significant to children fail to meet these high standards. When parents abandon their children or die, other adults—caretakers, foster parents, friends and members of the extended family—take their place, but not all fulfill the needs of the children. Some even abuse their acquired position of power.

> Our children...should not be left to drift in a world so laden with moral dangers. In the current state of society, children face a cruel fate. Millions and millions in country after country are dislocated socially. Children find themselves alienated by parents and other adults whether they live in conditions of wealth or poverty. This alienation has its roots in a selfishness that is born of materialism that is at the core of the godlessness seizing the hearts of people everywhere. The social dislocation of children in our time is a sure mark of a society

---

2000

176 'Abdu'l-Bahá, *Selections from the Writings of 'Abdu'l-Bahá.*

> in decline; this condition is not, however, confined to any race, class, nation or economic condition—it cuts across them all. It grieves our hearts to realize that in so many parts of the world children are employed as soldiers, exploited as laborers, sold into virtual slavery, forced into prostitution, made the objects of pornography, abandoned by parents centered on their own desires, and subjected to other forms of victimization too numerous to mention. Many such horrors are inflicted by the parents themselves upon their own children. The spiritual and psychological damage defies estimation. Our worldwide community cannot escape the consequences of these conditions. This realization should spur us all to urgent and sustained effort in the interests of children and the future...[177]

In many cases, families are broken up voluntarily or by the edicts of authorities and the children are turned over to other adults for supervision and education. Over many centuries, numerous Catholic families have enrolled their children in Catholic schools believing their children would be loved and well-educated. Muslim families likewise turned over control and education of their children to Islamic schools called madrasahs, and American Indian boarding schools housed and educated seized children to "assimilate" them culturally. The teachers and administrators of these schools, many of which had good intentions, often failed in their responsibilities and abused their positions of power.

Catholic Schools

Catholic schools, which date back to the early Middle Ages, were established and run by the Roman Catholic Church to educate clergy and provide basic education to the general population. Over

---

[177] The Universal House of Justice, "To the Bahá'ís of the World," Ridván 2000

the centuries, this purpose was conflated with the Catholic Church's mission to promote faith-based education. In an era of rational thinking, however, greater emphasis on teaching critical thinking skills is needed in schools and at home. Each child thinks differently, which is a bounty for humankind. To engage in an independent search for truth and not simply conform to the standards of a religious or civil institution is a signpost of humanity's coming of age.

A common justification for corporeal punishment in Catholic and other religious schools was the axiom, "Spare the rod and spoil the child," a rough paraphrasing of Proverbs 13:24 in the Old Testament. This was taken to mean that if a child who committed an offense was not beaten with a rod (or some other intimidating object) as punishment, that child would grow up to be spoiled. Unfortunately for many young students, this was a misinterpretation of the original guidance in which the rod mentioned was a staff that a shepherd used to guide the sheep as a group and was never used to beat the precious animals for fear of bruising them.

Today, Catholic schools play an important role in the education system of many countries by combining academic and religious education. Many Catholic schools have adapted their curricula and policies to better address contemporary issues and provide a safe and nurturing environment for their students. Like many institutions, however, Catholic schools have had their share of abuses and controversies.

In the past, Catholic schools were known for strict disciplinary practices including physical punishments such as caning or paddling students to maintain discipline. These practices have been widely condemned for their harmful physical and psychological effects on students. The sexual abuse of minors by priests and other clergy continues in the Catholic Church and its schools. These abuses were exposed in the late 20th and early 21st centuries, leading to widespread investigations and legal actions against the perpetrators and the Church.

Many former Catholic school students have reported emotional and psychological abuse by teachers, administrators and clergy including verbal insults, shaming and other forms of personal manipulation. And while many Catholic schools provide quality academic education, in some cases the emphasis on religious teachings and traditions has contributed to educational neglect in secular subjects. This can hinder students' broader academic development and preparation for the real world. It is still perhaps more common to ask our children how they feel rather than what they think, which too often teaches children that it is better to make decisions based on their emotions rather than on logical thinking.

The issues listed above are not representative of all Catholic schools. In recent years, the Church has attempted to address the problems of sexual abuse, implement child protection policies and hold accountable those responsible for any abuses. The experiences of the students, however, cannot be erased, nor can the lost opportunities for greater success in the world due to inadequate education.

Islamic Madrasahs

Madrasahs are Islamic institutions of learning and date back to the ninth century when the first madrasah was established in Baghdad. "Madrasah" is the Arabic word for "school." In Islamic cultures, madrasahs are primarily focused on teaching Islamic theology, law, and the Quran, which is the sacred text of Islam. Many reputable madrasahs provide quality education and contribute positively to their communities.

Many of the criticisms of madrasahs are similar to those of Catholic schools. Some believe that the almost singular focus on teaching religious topics at the expense of secular subjects such as mathematics, science and literature results in an unnecessarily narrow educational experience. The emphasis on rote memorization of religious texts, they complain, fails to foster critical thinking skills and understanding of the texts' meaning.

Most troubling is the potential of some madrasahs to adopt and promote extremist ideologies, which can lead to the radicalization of students who then acquire a skewed understanding of Islam that rationalizes hate and terrorism, domination over women and other extreme practices. Where madrasahs operate with minimal oversight or regulation, episodes of academic and physical abuse have been reported.

The problems cited above are not indicative of all madrasahs. In recent years, there have been efforts to reform and modernize madrasah education to address some of these criticisms and challenges.

American Indian Boarding Schools

American Indian boarding schools, today called residential schools, comprise a dark chapter in US history. The United States operated 408 boarding schools for indigenous children across thirty-seven states or then-territories... half of them likely supported by religious institutions.[178] The origins can be traced back to the Civilization Fund Act of 1819 that allocated funds to Christian missionary societies to develop schools for American Indian children. The purpose was less to provide academic education but rather to assimilate Indian children into Euro-American culture, language and customs. This was cultural genocide.

Between 1869 and the 1969, hundreds of thousands of American Indian children were literally kidnapped from their families and placed in boarding schools under the auspices of the federal government, which contracted with a number of religious organizations to operate them. These institutions, all of them Christian, include the Roman Catholic Church, the Christian Reformed Church, the Episcopal Church, the United Methodist Church, the Evangelical Lutheran Church and the Presbyterian Church. The government gave these

---

178 https://www.christianitytoday.com/news/2022/may/christian-native-american-boarding-schools-us-investigation.html.

churches tracts of reservation land to use for educational and missionary work and at times paid compensation for each indigenous child who entered a boarding school.

The religious organizations used these schools to Christianize "heathens" and civilize "savages" while simultaneously eradicating Indian cultural practices and languages, thus solidifying a predominantly "White" cultural. While the official aim was to promote cultural assimilation and education, these schools instead left behind a legacy of trauma, broken families, widespread abuse and cultural loss.

The boarding schools reeked of neglect and physical or sexual abuse reflecting the paternalistic and prejudiced attitudes prevalent in that time. The schools attempted to assimilate children by giving indigenous children English names, cutting their hair, even organizing them into units to perform military drills. They discouraged or prevented children from speaking indigenous languages or from engaging in their own spiritual and cultural practices. The trauma experienced by generations of Indian families reverberates today.

"The consequences of federal Indian boarding school policies—including the intergenerational trauma caused by forced family separation and cultural eradication, which were inflicted upon generations of children as young as four years old—are heartbreaking and undeniable," said Interior Secretary Deb Haaland, a member of the Pueblo of Laguna and the first Native American to serve as a Cabinet secretary.[179]

In recent years, there has been growing recognition of the need to confront this dark history and its legacy of abuse and cultural loss. Several of the Christian churches involved in the boarding schools have called for the US to establish a Truth and Healing Commission similar to one established in Canada due to similar abuses in that country's boarding schools.

---

179 https://www.christianitytoday.com/news/2022/may/christian-native-american-boarding-schools-us-investigation.html.

Education Can Be Misused

The three examples cited above could be expanded to a much longer list, but they point out that education, when its methods and goals are corrupted, can become a cause of great harm. Considering the manipulative use of shaming, insulting and beating children into compliance with the wishes of a teacher or school administrator, we wonder how things might have been different if the following guidance had been heeded:

> If a pupil is told that his intelligence is less than his fellow pupils, it is a very great drawback and handicap to his progress. He must be encouraged to advance...[180]

> The child must not be oppressed or censured because it is undeveloped; it must be patiently trained.[181]

The teachers and missionaries of the schools cited above seem to have ignored or been ignorant of the impressionability and vulnerability of the children in their care. Harsh punishments discourage learning, not encourage it. Physical and sexual abuse teach children that it is fine to get what you want through bullying, intimidation and abusive behavior. Do we want to groom children by example to become bullies and abusers?

> Children are even as a branch that is fresh and green; they will grow up in whatever way ye train them. Take the utmost care to give them high ideals and goals, so that once they come of age, they will cast their beams like brilliant candles on the world, and will not be defiled by lusts and passions in the way of animals, heedless and unaware, but instead will set their hearts

---

180 'Abdu'l-Bahá, *The Promulgation of World Peace*.
181 'Abdu'l-Bahá, *The Promulgation of World Peace*.

> on achieving everlasting honor and acquiring all the excellences of humankind.[182]

Is it fair to deprive children of an excellent academic education, which prepares them for gainful employment and the capacity to improve the world, in exchange for a narrow curriculum of primarily religious teaching?

> Exert every effort to acquire the various branches of knowledge and true understanding. Strain every nerve to achieve both material and spiritual accomplishments. Encourage the children from their earliest years to master every kind of learning, and make them eager to become skilled in every art… that each may earn world-wide fame in all branches of knowledge, science and the arts.[183]

> A scientific man is a true index and representative of humanity, for through processes of inductive reasoning and research he is informed of all that appertains to humanity, its status, conditions and happenings.[184]

What is the spiritual value of the mindless and ritualistic repetition of phrases and verses—even scriptural passages—to merely learn the pattern of words or recite them as a token of devotion without gaining knowledge of the deep meaning behind them? And cannot any ritual become divisive as some individuals fail to perform it, or perform it differently?

> All these divisions we see on all sides, all these disputes and opposition, are caused because men cling to rit-

---

182 'Abdu'l-Bahá, *Selections from the Writings of 'Abdu'l-Bahá*.
183 'Abdu'l-Bahá, from a Tablet, translated from the Persian.
184 'Abdu'l-Bahá, *The Promulgation of Universal Peace*, p. 20.

> ual and outward observances, and forget the simple, underlying truth.[185]

Women First

Women are encouraged in the Writings of the most recent wisdom tradition to study all branches of human knowledge and participate with men as equal partners in every field of human endeavor. To attain this goal…

> …most important of all is the education of girl children, for these girls will one day be mothers, and the mother is the first teacher of the child. In whatever way she reareth the child, so will the child become, and the results of that first training will remain with the individual throughout his entire life, and it would be most difficult to alter them. And how can a mother, herself ignorant and untrained, educate her child? It is therefore clear that the education of girls is of far greater consequence than that of boys. This fact is extremely important, and the matter must be seen to with the greatest energy and dedication.[186]

The truth of this statement was verified a half-century after it was written. For nearly thirty years, data has been available to show the correlation between a variety of crucial development indicators and the education of girls. From reductions in infant mortality, fertility, and the incidence of AIDS to improvements in the environment, it has been amply demonstrated that it is the mother's education that makes the difference[187] and that the positive effects increase with

---

185 'Abdu'l-Bahá, *Paris Talks*.
186 'Abdu'l-Bahá, from a Tablet, translated from the Persian.
187 "Making the Case for the Gender Variable: Women and the Wealth and Well-being of Nations," Technical Reports in Gender and Development, Office of

every additional year a girl stays in school. When all the benefits are considered, educating girls yields a higher rate of return than any other possible investment in the developing world. Why is it, then, that so many religious organizations and governments still restrict access to education for women?

Our Children

Sooner or later, humanity must understand that as the world shrinks, the education and spiritual awakening of children in all groups everywhere will affect the moral standards of our own. All children, then, should be regarded as part of our own family, and we must emphasize their education. Society is responsible to educate and raise the next generation so that no orphan or misplaced child will ever be left alone. It really does take a village to raise and educate a child.

In truth, the responsibility for educating the next generation belongs to the community, which must provide adequate funding to properly educate all of its children. This education must instill and reinforce rational thinking, which opens up to children all available knowledge, not just that which conforms to the parents' or community's point of view. Anything less than this is not education, but rather indoctrination.

Three Kinds of Education

Our latest wisdom tradition has identified three kinds of education: material, human and spiritual[188]. Material education concerns itself with the progress and development of the body—teaching people how to improve physical well-being, which includes better nutrition and hygiene, better family health and greater capacity to earn and provide food, shelter and clothing.

Women in Development, US Agency for International Development, 1989.
  188 'Abdu'l-Bahá, *Some Answered Questions*, Part 1: On the Influence of the Prophets in the Evolutions of Humanity: "3. The Need for an Educator"

Human education concerns civilization and progress in those activities that are essential to humankind as distinct from the animal world, such as knowledge of commerce, the sciences and arts, and the understanding of institutions and their policies.

Spiritual or moral education addresses values and shapes character. It largely determines to what end an individual will use the knowledge he or she acquires. Spiritual or moral education is almost never seen outside of parochial schools or religious institutions. It is shunned in most developed countries as irrelevant or intrusive to modern education. It is, however, the one kind of education that asserts the dignity of the human spirit in all its diversity and formalizes its relationship to the Divine.

Such universal human values as trustworthiness, honesty, courtesy, generosity, respect and kindness are rapidly disappearing from our increasingly belligerent and fractured world. Through moral or character education, whether formalized in structured programs or provided informally by wise and caring family or community members, that which is valued by society and gives meaning to life is transmitted to succeeding generations.[189]

Few would disagree with the latest wisdom tradition that all three kinds of education are important.

Material Education

Education about our material bodies is important as long as we abide in a material existence. We are mainly dependent on ourselves for maintaining our health and staying alive to help achieve an ever-advancing society.

> The human body is in reality very weak; there is no physical body more delicately constituted. One mos-

---

[189] "Educating Girls and Women," Statement to the 39th session of the United Nations Commission on the Status of Women Item 2 of the provisional agenda: Priority Themes: Development: Promotion of literacy, education and training, including technological skills.

> quito will distress it; the smallest quantity of poison will destroy it; if respiration ceases for a moment, it will die. What instrument could be weaker and more delicate? A blade of grass severed from the root may live an hour, whereas a human body deprived of its forces may die in one minute. But in the proportion that the human body is weak, the spirit of man is strong. It can control natural phenomena; it is a supernatural power which transcends all contingent beings. It has immortal life, which nothing can destroy or pervert.[190]

But we are not responsible only for our own material existence. If we are parents, we must also do our best to care for them physically as well as spiritually.

> ...if a child is not properly cared for at the beginning of life, so that he doth not develop a sound body and his constitution doth not flourish as it ought, his body will remain feeble, and whatever is done afterward will take little effect. This matter of protecting the health of the child is essential, for sound health leadeth to insights and sense perceptions, and then the child, as he learneth sciences, arts, skills, and the civilities of life, will duly develop his powers....[191]

In this age, spiritual enlightenment must go hand in hand with material education, which alone cannot make the world happy.

Human Education

Because humans live a material existence, gaining knowledge about that existence is essential. This existence relies on scientific laws and is enhanced by artistic expressions of many kinds. It is impossible to

---

190 'Abdu'l-Bahá, *The Promulgation of Universal Peace*.
191 *Lights of Guidance*, (From a previously untranslated Tablet by Abdu'l-Bahá)

fathom. Human education, then, is the exploration and acquiring of knowledge about this existence, and it has been made clear to us that we have an obligation to acquire as much of this knowledge as we can and use it to help achieve an ever-advancing civilization.

> Observe carefully how education and the arts of civilization bring honor, prosperity, independence and freedom to a government and its people.[192]

> Arts, crafts and sciences uplift the world of being, and are conducive to its exaltation. Knowledge is as wings to man's life, and a ladder for his ascent. Its acquisition is incumbent upon everyone. The knowledge of such sciences, however, should be acquired as can profit the peoples of the earth, and not those which begin with words and end with words.

> In truth, knowledge is a veritable treasure for man, and a source of glory, of bounty, of joy, of exaltation, of cheer and gladness unto him. Happy the man that cleaveth unto it, and woe betide the heedless.[193]

> At the outset of every endeavor, it is incumbent to look to the end of it. Of all the arts and sciences, set the children to studying those which will result in advantage to man, will ensure his progress and elevate his rank. Thus the noisome odors of lawlessness will be dispelled, and thus through the high endeavors of the nation's leaders, all will live cradled, secure and in peace.[194]

---

192 'Abdu'l-Bahá, *The Secret of Divine Civililzation*.
193 Bahá'u'lláh, *Epistle to the Son of the Wolf*.
194 Bahá'u'lláh, *Tablets of Bahá'u'lláh, Lawh-i-Maqsúd*.

Spiritual or Moral Education

As a matter of principle, our most recent wisdom tradition gives priority to spiritual and moral education over the other kinds.

> Good behaviour and high moral character must come first, for unless the character be trained, acquiring knowledge will only prove injurious. Knowledge is praiseworthy when it is coupled with ethical conduct and virtuous character; otherwise it is a deadly poison, a frightful danger.[195]

> The purport is this, that to train the character of humankind is one of the weightiest commandments of God, and the influence of such training is the same as that which the sun exerteth over tree and fruit. Children must be most carefully watched over, protected and trained; in such consisteth true parenthood and parental mercy.[196]

One reason that spiritual education or development is so important to achieving an ever-advancing civilization is that humankind is just now stepping onto the stage of our spiritual potential. In other words, *we ain't seen nothin' yet* compared to our full spiritual capacity.

> Man is in the ultimate degree of materiality and the beginning of spirituality; that is, he is at the end of imperfection and the beginning of perfection. He is at the furthermost degree of darkness and the beginning of the light. That is why the station of man is said to be the end of night and the beginning of day, meaning

---

[195] Bahá'u'lláh, 'Abdu'l-Bahá, Shoghi Effendi, *Scholarship*.
[196] 'Abdu'l-Bahá, from a Tablet, translated from the Persian.

> that he encompasses all the degrees of imperfection and that he potentially possesses all the degrees of perfection. He has both an animal side and an angelic side, and the role of the educator is to so train human souls that the angelic side may overcome the animal.[197]

> Strain every nerve to acquire both inner and outer perfections, for the fruit of the human tree hath ever been and will ever be perfections both within and without. It is not desirable that a man be left without knowledge or skills, for he is then but a barren tree. Then, so much as capacity and capability allow, ye needs must deck the tree of being with fruits such as knowledge, wisdom, spiritual perception and eloquent speech.[198]

---

197 'Abdu'l-Bahá, *Some Answered Questions*, p. 235

198 Bahá'u'lláh, from a Tablet, translated from the Persian, available at: https://bit.ly/4b71Bfd

Chapter 9:
Economic Justice

Economic Inequality Is a Growing Problem

Ask ten people if they see an unfair disparity between poverty and wealth in their country and you will likely get ten affirmations. Few would claim that a society in which a few have enormous wealth and many live in extreme poverty is fair and just. A wide disparity of wealth is a major cause of disunity as the poor disparagingly think of the rich as an entitled and elite bunch that "hoards" material resources, and the rich often view the poor as self-imposed victims of their own ignorance or lack of ambition.

In the US, the Federal Reserve data shows that as of the last quarter of 2021, the top 1 percent of households held nearly a third (32.3 percent) of the country's wealth. By contrast, the bottom 50 percent collectively held just 2.6 percent.[199]

The Washington Center of Equitable Growth reported in 2019 that the bottom 50 percent of wealth owners experienced no net wealth growth since 1989. The top 1 percent, however, saw their wealth

---

199   https://en.wikipedia.org/wiki/Wealth_inequality_in_the_United_States. Retrieved July 22, 2023.

grow by 300 percent over that same period.[200] Thus, the disparity of wealth is growing at an alarming rate for those not in the top 1 percent.

The Pew Research Center in 2020 summarized the phenomenon in these words:

> The growth in income in recent decades has tilted to upper-income households. At the same time, the U.S. middle class[201], which once comprised the clear majority of Americans, is shrinking. Thus, a greater share of the nation's aggregate income is now going to upper-income households and the share going to middle- and lower-income households is falling.[202]

Many economists claim the rise in economic inequality in the US is tied to several factors including technological change, globalization, the decline of unions and the eroding value of the minimum wage. Whatever the causes, however, the unimpeded velocity of inequality since 1980 often causes people in the lower rungs of the economic ladder to have diminished economic opportunity and mobility, a phenomenon referred to as The Great Gatsby Curve.[203] This Curve illustrates the connection between the concentration of wealth in one generation and the ability of those in the next generation to move up the economic ladder compared to their parents.

---

200 "The Federal Reserve's new distributional financial accounts provide telling data on growing U.S. wealth and income inequality". http://equitablegrowth.org. August 22, 2019. Retrieved February 17, 2020.

201 "Middle-income" Americans are adults whose annual household income is two-thirds to double the national median, after incomes have been adjusted for household size. Lower-income households have incomes less than 67 percent of the median and upper-income households have incomes that are more than double the median.

202 https://www.pewresearch.org/social-trends/2020/01/09/trends-in-income-and-wealth-inequality/. Retrieved July 22, 2023.

203 https://obamawhitehouse.archives.gov/blog/2013/06/11/what-great-gatsby-curve. Retrieved July 22, 2023.

Other analysts have highlighted inequality's negative impact on the political influence of the disadvantaged, geographic segregation by income, diminished economic growth, social and political instability[204] and threats to environmental sustainability.[205] On a more personal level, inequality can lead to shorter, unhealthier and unhappier lives including increases in teenage pregnancy, violence and obesity.

Calamities Foster Economic Redistribution

When calamities strike, redistribution of material resources usually follows. In the US, the Great Depression gave birth to the New Deal—sweeping government programs and reforms intended to provide immediate relief for the "forgotten man."[206] Two world wars saw the expansion and consolidation of the modern welfare state, which was designed to provide a "cradle-to-grave" safety net through health, education, housing and retirement benefits.

For today's generation, the Great Recession of 2008 and the coronavirus pandemic exposed alarming social and economic inequalities and reinvigorated debate about the causes and consequences of economic instability. Stunned governments embarked on unprecedented levels of social spending, hundreds of billions to prevent the failure of banks in 2008/9 and trillions to prevent the grave effects of mass unemployment in 2020.

Nevertheless, as we have seen, the distribution of material resources has grown ever more unequal. According to one social historian, inequality has risen since the Stone Age and only four forces—the "Four Horsemen of Leveling"—have ever managed to lower it: pandemics, mass warfare, revolution and state collapse.[207]

---

204 Alberto Alesina and Roberto Perotti, "Income Distribution, Political Instability and Investment," European Economic Review 40, no.6 (1996):1203-1228.

205 See the annual reports of the Global Commission on the Economy and Climate.

206 Franklin D. Roosevelt's speech on the "forgotten man" on the eve of his announcing the New Deal. Accessed at https://bit.ly/3f387Xy on June 9, 2020.

207 Scheidel, Walter, *The Great Leveler: Violence and the History of Inequality*

It may surprise some that religion provides important insights and explicit guidance about this issue and the ultimate solution. The latest wisdom tradition calls the inordinate disparity between rich and poor…

> …a source of acute suffering [that] keeps the world in a state of instability, virtually on the brink of war. Few societies have dealt effectively with this situation. The solution calls for the combined application of spiritual, moral and practical approaches.[208]

Of course, most agree that extreme economic inequality is bad. But is there a rational concept of how much inequality may be good? Put another way, can any level of inequality be considered acceptable or justified? Our most recent wisdom tradition has set out coherent principles related to distributional issues that can be connected to today's economic issues.

Principles Regarding (In)Equality

The latest wisdom tradition explicitly condemns the extreme economic divide between the wealthiest and poorest in society. It also clarifies that the distribution of wealth it calls for should not be understood as absolute equality.

> …social inequality is the inevitable outcome of the natural inequality of men. Human beings are different in ability and should, therefore, be different in their social and economic standing. Extremes of wealth and poverty should, however, be totally abolished. Those whose brains have contributed to the creation and

---

from the Stone Age to the Twenty-First Century.

208 Universal House of Justice, letter of October 1985 to the peoples of the world, titled "The Promise of World Peace". Available at www.bahai.org/r/267204466.

> improvement of the means of production must be fairly rewarded, though these means may be owned and controlled by others.[209]

Divine Justice

According to a principle referred to as divine justice, perfect economic equality among all the members of humankind is not only undesirable but unattainable. The Writings explain that by divine justice...

> ...[i]t is not meant that all will be equal, for inequality in degree and capacity is a property of nature. Necessarily there will be rich people and also those who will be in want of their livelihood, but in the aggregate community there will be equalization and readjustment of values and interests.[210]

What matters more than absolute financial equality is an equal chance to succeed, which is called for in these words: "justness of opportunity for all."[211]

Moderation

The solution to many of the economic problems afflicting humanity is surprisingly simple—*moderation*. When moderation in all things is not practiced and extreme views take root, all aspects of social needs and global requirements are threatened with collapse.

> If carried to excess, civilization will prove as prolific a source of evil as it had been of goodness when kept within the restraints of moderation.[212]

---

209 Shoghi Effendi, quoted in *Lights of Guidance*, "A 1935 letter written on behalf of Shoghi Effendi to an individual believer," January 26, 1935.
210 'Abdu'l-Bahá, *The Promulgation of Universal Peace*.
211 'Abdu'l-Bahá, *The Promulgation of Universal Peace*.
212 Bahá'u'lláh, *Gleanings from the Writings of Bahá'u'lláh*.

The pragmatic vision of our latest wisdom tradition is that a certain amount of unequal wealth is natural, even desirable, because incentives for greater rewards can provide motivation for greater achievements. But extreme disparities in wealth are unjust and destructive to individuals and society in general.

> Every human being has the right to live; they have a right to rest, and to a certain amount of well-being. As a rich man is able to live in his palace surrounded by luxury and the greatest comfort, so should a poor man be able to have the necessaries of life. Nobody should die of hunger; everybody should have sufficient clothing; one man should not live in excess while another has no possible means of existence.[213]

Since this sought-after condition does not exist at present, an update is necessary in civil and spiritual laws as well as in the hearts of individuals. The "readjustment in the economic conditions of mankind" that this latest wisdom tradition envisions will be such that...

> ...in the future there will not be the abnormally rich nor the abject poor. The rich will enjoy the privilege of this new economic condition as well as the poor, for owing to certain provisions and restrictions they will not be able to accumulate so much as to be burdened by its management, while the poor will be relieved from the stress of want and misery.[214]

On the surface, this rational view seems quite simple, but striking the correct balance in the distribution of wealth has proven immensely difficult as demonstrated in the statistics leading off this

---

213 'Abdu'l-Bahá, *Paris Talks*, pp. 133-134.
214 'Abdu'l-Bahá, *The Promulgation of Universal Peace*.

chapter. It is not necessary to demonize wealth to achieve this balance. The Teachings regard wealth as necessary and desirable, a natural consequence of individual achievement, provided it is acquired honestly and used in part for philanthropic purposes, which is the sign of a mature global view.

> Wealth is praiseworthy in the highest degree, if it is acquired by an individual's own efforts and the grace of God, in commerce, agriculture, art and industry, and if it be expended for philanthropic purposes. Above all, if a judicious and resourceful individual should initiate measures which would universally enrich the masses of the people, there could be no undertaking greater than this… If, however, a few have inordinate riches while the rest are impoverished, and no fruit or benefit accrues from that wealth, then it is only a liability to its possessor.[215]

On the other side of the equation, the latest wisdom tradition prohibits asceticism and discourages adopting austere lifestyles. In a letter of guidance written to a couple pledging to adopt an extremely austere lifestyle so the saved money could be donated to their Faith, the guidance was clear and concise.

> Let them act with moderation and not impose hardship upon themselves. We would like them both to enjoy a life that is well-pleasing.[216]

According to this wisdom tradition, the rational concept of moderation applies not only to financial matters but to everything in life, explaining that those who seek to follow its Teachings…

---

215 Abdu'l-Bahá, *Secret of Divine Civilization*, p. 24
216 Bahá'u'lláh, quoted in the compilation entitled *Huqúqulláh—The Right of God*, Selection No. 19. Available at https://bit.ly/3fpYphM.

> ...are enjoined to use moderation in all things, and to seek the Golden mean[217]...[218]

Economic Justice Based on Interconnectedness

The latest wisdom tradition points out that the extreme disparity of wealth and poverty and its solution—economic justice—are issues based on our interconnectedness. To what extent is extreme wealth a cause and perhaps also a consequence of extreme poverty? Do policies that allow and possibly promote extreme concentrations of wealth make it easier for the disadvantaged to fall into destitution?

> The welfare of any segment of humanity is inextricably bound up with the welfare of the whole. Humanity's collective life suffers when any one group thinks of its own well-being in isolation from that of its neighbors.[219]

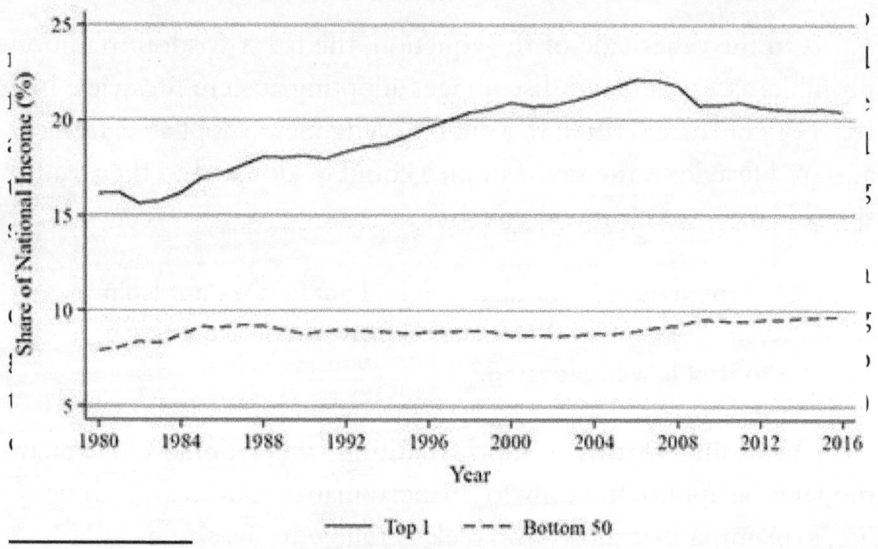

---

217 Aristotle's "golden mean'" is his theory that excellence lies in the middle way between two extreme states: excess and deficiency.

218 Shoghi Effendi, *Messages to the Indian Subcontinent*.

219 Universal House of Justice, letter of 1 March 2017 to the Bahá'ís of the World regarding economic life. Available at www.bahai.org/r/934375828.

The previous chart demonstrates differences in *levels* and *trends* between top and bottom earners. With respect to levels, those in the top 1 percent of income distribution earn about 10 percent more of national income than those in the bottom 50 percent. In addition, increases for top earners are trending at three times the rate. Between 1980 and 2016, those in the top 1 percent of the income distribution increased their share of national income by 4.4 percent. For those in the bottom 50 percent, their share of national income increased by just 1.5 percent over the same period.

This chart casts significant doubt on the assertion—often used to justify tax cuts for the wealthy—that rises in income at the very top provide wealth, opportunity, and incentives for those at the bottom. While a rising tide may lift all boats, structuring the economy to funnel wealth upward does not. Consequently, economic justice requires the rules that regulate the economy to be fair and not tilted to enrich a particular segment of society.[220]

Legislative Readjustment

The most recent wisdom tradition has identified the need to recalibrate our system of economic justice.

> This inequality of portion and privilege is one of the deep and vital problems of human society. That there is need of an equalization and apportionment by which all may possess the comforts and privileges of life is evident. The remedy must be legislative readjustment of conditions.[221]

The mechanism through which society expresses its values regarding the social order is public policy, and the power of policy

---

[220] The chart its analysis are extracted from Navid Sabet, "Is Economic Justice Possible?" available at https://bahaiworld.bahai.org/library/is-economic-justice-possible/.

[221] 'Abdu'l-Bahá, *The Promulgation of World Peace*.

to shape societies must not be undervalued. Unlike the natural universe, prevailing economic theories on which most public fiscal policy is based are not grounded in universal, immutable laws. They are merely social constructs based on analysis of how humans have responded to policies and events in the past and extrapolating from there. Of course, as human behavior matures, it changes over time to the consternation of economists when they recognize it.

Nevertheless, a nonpartisan analysis of data shows that public policy can indeed shape the economy to achieve a certain social outcome. This means that hyper-concentration of wealth is either a choice made by policymakers or an accident of bad policies. *It is not an inevitability.* The conclusion, then, must be that legislation resulting in economic injustice is either designed to be purposely immoral, in that it consciously favors the wealthy over the poor, or is inept, which means that when the flaws are identified they can be fixed.

> There is no justification for continuing to perpetuate structures, rules, and systems that manifestly fail to serve the interests of all peoples. The teachings of the [Bahá'í] Faith leave no room for doubt: there is an inherent moral dimension to the generation, distribution, and utilization of wealth and resources.[222]

This moral dimension suggests that policy should be designed to serve the interests of everybody. Implementing novel ways to serve the economic interests of the few at the expense of the many is a characteristic of humanity's collective childhood, not of its coming of age.

The Power of Personal Participation

The creation of public policies that reflect the interests of everyone does not occur without "everyone" making their interests known to policymakers. A prominent political theorist wrote, "A key

---

222 Universal House of Justice, letter of 1 March 2017 to the Bahá'ís of the World regarding economic life. Available at www.bahai.org/r/934375828.

characteristic of democracy is the continuing responsiveness of the government to the preferences of its citizens, considered as political equals."[223] One way the government does this is by paying attention to who votes.

Unfortunately, voter turnout in recent years has declined in many countries and this decrease is often along class lines. Numerous studies have shown that voters are typically better educated, wealthier and more informed politically than non-voters. These same characteristics correlate strongly with preferences for redistribution.[224]

Slumping voter turnout implies that the preferences of the wealthy may be over-represented, which places less pressure on policymakers to work for redistribution. Supporting this inference, academic scholarship has shown a robust relationship between the rate of voter turnout and the size of government spending on redistributive policies. These studies have found that higher turnout across countries leads to higher top marginal tax rates,[225] welfare expenditure and the political leaning of the party in power,[226] and social spending in non-welfare categories such as education and health.[227]

Within countries, various episodes of voter enfranchisement have been studied to show that governments systematically tar-

---

223 Robert A. Dahl, *Polyarchy: Participation and Opposition*.

224 See, for example, Valentino Larcinese, "Voting over Redistribution and the Size of the Welfare State: The Role of Turnout," Political Studies 55 (2007):568-585; Martin Gilens, "Inequality and Democratic Responsiveness," Public Opinion Quarterly 69, no. 5(2005): 778-796; Benjamen I. Page et al, "Democracy and the Policy Preferences of Wealthy Americans," Perspectives on Politics 11, no. 1(2013): 51-73.

225 Navid Sabet, "Turning Out for Redistribution: The Effect of Voter Turnout on Top Marginal Tax Rates," Munich Discussion Paper no. 2016-13 Accessed 22 August 2020: https://epub.ub.uni-muenchen.de/72625/.

226 Alexander M. Hicks and Duane H. Swank, "Politics, Institutions, and Welfare Spending in Industrialised Democracies, 1960-1982," American Political Science Review 86, no. 3 (1992): 658–674.

227 Peter H. Lindert, "What Limits Social Spending?" Explorations in Economic History 33 (1996):1–34.

get resources to serve the economic interests of the newly enfranchised group. This appears to be true of African Americans,[228] women,[229] lesser educated citizens,[230] and undocumented migrants.[231] [232]

Put simply, if lower income citizens are less likely to vote, public economic policy is less likely to favor their preferences. Measures to promote voter turnout help ensure that markets are structured to serve the interests of all people. Some reporters, such as Fareed Zakaria, believe that political systems around the world are moving toward dictatorships or Theocracies, which means we may have a need for a new standard of democracy in which everyone's rights are met and no one is left behind.

While the latest wisdom tradition does not seek political power—it discourages members from participation in partisan politics because, by definition, partisanship is divisive—it urges its enrolled members to vote in civil elections…

> …as long as they do not have to identify themselves with any party in order to do so. In this connection, they view government as a system for maintaining the welfare and orderly progress of a society, and they undertake, one and all, to observe the laws of the land

---

228 Elizabeth U. Cascio and Ebonya L. Washington, "Valuing the Vote: The Redistribution of Voting Rights and State Funds Following the Voting Rights Act of 1965," The Quarterly Journal of Economics 129, no.1(2914):379-433.

229 Grant Miller, "Women's Suffrage, Political Responsiveness, and Child Survival in American History," The Quarterly Journal of Economics 123, no.3 (2008):1287–1327.

230 Thomas Fujiwara, "Voting Technology, Political Responsiveness, and Infant Health: Evidence from Brazil," Econometrica 83, no. 2 (2015): 423–464.

231 Navid Sabet and Christoph Winter, 2019. "Legal Status and Local Spending: The Distributional Consequences of the 1986 IRCA," CESifo Working Paper Series No. 7611, CESifo. Accessed 22 August 2020: https://www.cesifo.org/DocDL/cesifo1_wp7611_0.pdf.

232 Navid Sabet, "Is Economic Justice Possible?" available at https://bahai-world.bahai.org/library/is-economic-justice-possible/.

> in which they reside, without allowing their inner religious beliefs to be violated.[233]

Profit Sharing

Because ends should be consistent with means, achieving moderate social and economic outcomes requires moderate policies. The newest wisdom tradition asks all governments to unite and form an assembly to discuss the distribution of resources and enact regulations and policies so that "neither the capitalists suffer from enormous losses nor the laborers become needy. In the utmost moderation they should make the law."[234]

> It is preferable, then, that some measure of moderation be achieved, and by moderation is meant the enactment of such laws and regulations as would prevent the unwarranted concentration of wealth in the hands of the few and satisfy the essential needs of the many. For instance, the factory owners reap a fortune every day, but the wage the poor workers are paid cannot even meet their daily needs: This is most unfair, and assuredly no just man can accept it.

> Therefore, laws and regulations should be enacted which would grant the workers both a daily wage and a share in a fourth or fifth of the profits of the factory in accordance with its means, or which would have the workers equitably share in some other way in the profits with the owners. For the capital and the management come from the latter and the toil and labour from the former. The workers could either be granted a wage that adequately meets their daily needs, as well as a

---

233 Universal House of Justice, "Non-Involvement in Partisan Politics"
234 'Abdu'l-Bahá. *The Promulgation of Universal Peace.*

> right to a share in the revenues of the factory when they are injured, incapacitated, or unable to work, or else a wage could be set that allows the workers to both satisfy their daily needs and save a little for times of weakness and incapacity.[235]

An interesting measure suggested here is profit sharing—sharing between a fourth to a fifth of the profits of the business "in accordance with its means"—as part of a nation's "laws and regulations." Another is setting wages according to need, not just market prices—a subtle but significant change from most current practices.

Collective Wealth

The latest wisdom tradition also proposes that legislation implement progressive taxation based on needs so that...

> ...[e]ach person in the community whose income is equal to his individual producing capacity shall be exempt from taxation. But if his income is greater than his needs, he must pay a tax until an adjustment is effected. That is to say, a man's capacity for production and his needs will be equalized and reconciled through taxation. If his production exceeds he will pay a tax; if his necessities exceed his production he shall receive an amount sufficient to equalize or adjust. Therefore, taxation will be proportionate to capacity and production and there will be no poor in the community.[236]

Most government revenues today come from income taxes. Strangely, while individuals have become richer in many countries, their governments have become poorer when considering the net

---

235 'Abdu'l-Bahá. *Some Answered Questions*.

236 Abdu'l-Bahá. *The Promulgation of Universal Peace*, p. 217. In other writings 'Abdu'l-Bahá provides examples where, depending on an individual's surplus, they may be taxed anywhere between 25 and 50 percent.

share of public and private capital held in each country. For example, in 2015, the value of net public wealth in Germany was 18 percent of national income. However, private wealth was 420 percent of national income. In the US that same year, net public wealth was 17 percent and private capital 500 percent of national income. This shows a tremendous disparity in favor of private capital compared to public capital. According to author Navid Sabet:

> This unequal ownership of capital—between private citizens and the state—may also explain rising inequality. In the 1980s, there were demonstrably large transfers of public to private wealth in nearly all countries. While national wealth has substantially increased, public wealth is now negative or close to zero in rich countries. Arguably this limits the ability of governments to tackle inequality. But more than that, it eats away at things like trust and social cohesion, so essential for a stable, prosperous society. When governments... consistently take more from the poor than the rich, establishing and maintaining trust in public institutions becomes increasingly difficult.[237]

This analysis leads to an interesting conclusion consistent with statements previously presented by the newest wisdom tradition. Clearly, the strategy should be *not* to punish wealth but to avoid privatization and consequently the accompanying polarization of society, whereby only those with means can afford quality education, healthcare and other essentials.

One way, then, in which governments could accomplish the goals set forth by the most recent wisdom tradition is to create a combination of policies aimed at both redistribution and predistribution. *Redistribution* of wealth would involve a steeply

---

[237] Navid Sabet, "Is Economic Justice Possible?" available at https://bahai-world.bahai.org/library/is-economic-justice-possible/.

progressive tax on income and on wealth, plus effective corporate taxation to curb tax avoidance. *Pre-distribution* would incorporate sufficient social spending to fund a modern, social welfare state with ample investments in healthcare and education to ensure that everyone has an equal chance to succeed. In addition, labor market regulations would prevent extreme wage dispersion to top executives.

Such a strategy is only one example of how the economic justice concept of this latest wisdom tradition could become a reality once public sentiment for it reached critical mass. The goals and values have been clearly stated. What remains is to achieve agreement that the goals are worth the effort.

Aspiring toward a Just Economy

Great advances in human coordination have come from the market economy. The complex global supply chain allows products to be assembled from parts made in many countries and then arrive efficiently at one's doorstep or loading dock.

Simultaneously, many nations have made economic growth the dominating process of human life. Organizing society to serve the needs of the economy, however, has significantly altered the way in which we understand human nature and relationships. Achieving a truly just social order will require more than a handful of cosmetic changes to how taxes are set and who receives which financial transfers. It will also require a deep examination of how market-obsessed societies have influenced human behavior and how we can reconstruct relationships in light of spiritual principles.

Personal Consumption

A deliberate goal of the twentieth century global development effort was to push developing nations through various preparatory stages to be ready for an age of high mass consumption.[238] To sustain high

---

[238] Walt W. Rostow, The Stages of Economic Growth: A Non-Communist Manifesto. (New York: Cambridge University Press, 1990).

levels of economic growth, attention was focused on convincing people to satisfy their needs and also their *wants* in the marketplace. Economists and their marketing partners explicitly stimulated and expanded people's *wants*.

At the time, the experts believed "wants are limited because the goods one knows about and can use are limited."[239] Increase people's wants and you can increase consumption, they thought, and consequently demand for goods and services will increase. With this logic, they were certain the right strategy for societies lay in spreading knowledge about new goods, which was "the key to the expansion of wants."[240] This probably was not the beginning of a long simmering "materialism," as it would become known, but certainly was the combustion point.

For anyone concerned about an ever-advancing society, the difference between needs and wants is economically profound. Satisfying the needs of an individual whose main purpose is to serve others and contribute to a more just society requires different economic arrangements than those that will satisfy individuals who develop new *wants* every day. The words of our most recent wisdom tradition leave a penetrating influence:

> O Son of Man! Thou dost wish for gold and I desire thy freedom from it. Thou thinkest thyself rich in its possession, and I recognize thy wealth in thy sanctity therefrom. By My life! This is My knowledge, and that is thy fancy; how can My way accord with thine?[241]

Of course, there is no universal set of needs for all people at all times. One may require a suit for work, but how many are needed, and of what quality? And does the suit need a designer label? This is not to say that only basic needs are good and all forms of desire—

---

239 Arthur Lewis, *The Theory of Economic Growth*.
240 Arthur Lewis, *The Theory of Economic Growth*.
241 Bahá'u'lláh. *The Hidden Words from the Arabic* No. 56.

those pesky *wants*— are bad. But without reflection on our personal consumption habits, we may yield needlessly to the temptations of the market while foregoing opportunities to refine our higher nature. Perhaps the issue is one of awareness. How conscious are we of what we consume and why?

> "Managing one's financial affairs in accordance with spiritual principles is an indispensable dimension of a life lived coherently. It is a matter of conscience, a way in which commitment to the betterment of the world is translated into practice."[242]

Compassion and Love

Evaluating a person's worth by their economic status is common in societies focused on acquisition and consumption. This characteristic must be eradicated if an economy based on spiritual principles is to be built.

> To view the worth of an individual chiefly in terms of how much one can accumulate and how many goods one can consume relative to others is wholly alien to [the newest wisdom tradition].[243]

This implies the need for a change of attitude toward the poor.

> No deed of man is greater before God, than helping the poor. Each one of you must have great consideration for the poor and render them assistance.[244]

---

242 Universal House of Justice, letter of 29 December 2015 to the Conference of the Continental Board of Counsellors. Available at www.bahai.org/r/521400059.

243 Universal House of Justice, letter of 1 March 2017 to the Bahá'ís of the World regarding economic life. Available at www.bahai.org/r/476802933.

244 'Abdu'l-Bahá. *The Promulgation of Universal Peace*.

> The rich too must be merciful to the poor, contributing from willing hearts to their needs without being forced or compelled to do so.[245]

Achieving this level of compassion requires love.

> Hearts must be so cemented together, love must become so dominant that the rich shall most willingly extend assistance to the poor and take steps to establish these economic adjustments permanently. If it is accomplished in this way, it will be most praiseworthy because then it will be for the sake of God and in the pathway of His service. For example, it will be as if the rich inhabitants of a city should say, "It is neither just nor lawful that we should possess great wealth while there is abject poverty in this community," and then willingly give their wealth to the poor, retaining only as much as will enable them to live comfortably.[246]

Introducing such idealistic concepts into public discourse today may seem difficult. In trying to establish a conversation, though, it may be helpful to note that these ideals have received intellectual support. An influential economic article noted this:

> Almost all economic models assume that all people are exclusively pursuing their material self-interest and do not care about "social" goals per se. This may be true for some (maybe many) people, but it is certainly not true for everybody. By now we have substantial evidence suggesting that fairness motives affect the behavior of many people.[247]

---

245 'Abdu'l-Bahá. *The Promulgation of Universal Peace*.
246 'Abdu'l-Bahá. *The Promulgation of Universal Peace*.
247 Ernest Fehr and Klaus M. Schmidt, "A Theory of Fairness, Competition and Cooperation," Quarterly Journal of Economics 114, no.3 (1999):817-868.

In recent decades, the economics of altruism have flourished. Many examples show human beings to be more than calculating, self-interested beings as proposed by initial, primitive economic models. Evidence now demonstrates that many are motivated as much by considerations of fairness and cooperation as by selfishness. To that list the authors would add love and compassion.

Those who seek an economy based on the principles of justice and equity do not object to efforts that improve material conditions or increase wealth and income, but rather that such efforts have come at the expense of an expanded view of human nature that includes a spiritual dimension.

As they relate to economic fairness and justice, the policies we choose matter. So do the candidates we elect, the goods and services we consume, our understanding of human nature and the purpose of our existence. All these have cumulative effects on the way that markets and their outcomes are structured. For everyone who wants to help bring about an ever-advancing society with economic justice for all, our most recent wisdom tradition advises this:

> **Every choice [that person] makes leaves a trace, and the moral duty to lead a coherent life demands that one's economic decisions be in accordance with lofty ideals.**[248]

Through moderate yet bold legislative adjustment and a spiritually awakened humanity, material and spiritual prosperity can coexist.

---

248 Universal House of Justice, letter of 1 March 2017 to the Baháʼís of the World regarding economic life. Available at www.bahai.org/r/904550633,

Chapter 10:
Social Justice and Action

An Ancient Concept

The concept of justice has pervaded religious and philosophical texts since the earliest times and transcends cultural and temporal boundaries. It has been a cornerstone of human societies and ethical frameworks since humans were first able to imagine such things, providing humanity with a moral compass that directs societies toward fairness, equity and harmonious coexistence. For millennia, the complex and multifaceted nature of justice has been dissected, debated and interpreted to reflect the commonalities as well as the diversity of human thought.

Abrahamic Religions

In Judaism, Zoroastrianism, Christianity and Islam, often referred to as the Abrahamic religions, justice is often presented as an attribute of the divine passed down to humanity in the form of laws and ethical guidelines for human conduct. The Hebrew Bible, for instance, emphasizes the importance of righteousness and impartiality in judgments explained in passages such as:

> **Follow justice and justice alone, so that you may live and possess the land the LORD your God is giving you.**[249]

For Zoroastrians, the Law of Asha is the principle of righteousness or "rightness" by which all things are exactly what they should be. Righteousness is a synonym for justice. In their most basic prayer, which is repeated daily, Zoroastrians affirm this Law of Asha by saying:

> **Righteousness is the highest virtue. Happiness to him who is righteous for the sake of righteousness.**

In Christianity, the teachings of Jesus underscore forgiveness, mercy, and the inherent worth of every individual, forming the foundation for a just society. In the New Testament, Jesus is quoted as saying that the pursuit of justice is worth persecution.

> **Blessed are those who are persecuted because of righteousness, for theirs is the kingdom of heaven.**[250]

Islam also champions justice, as emphasized by the Quran's injunctions to establish justice even if it goes against one's own interests.

> **O believers! Stand firm for justice as witnesses for Allah even if it is against yourselves, your parents, or close relatives. Be they rich or poor, Allah is best to ensure their interests. So do not let your desires cause you to deviate 'from justice'.**[251]

---

249 *Bible*, Deuteronomy 16:20, New International Version.
250 *Bible*, Matthew 5:10, New International Version.
251 *Quran*, Surah An-Nisa Ayat 135.

Eastern Religions

Eastern religious traditions also emphasize justice but with unique perspectives. In Buddhism, the concept of karma highlights the notion that actions have consequences, implying that justice is a natural outcome of one's deeds. Hinduism emphasizes the importance of righteousness and the dilemma of its opposite condition, unrighteousness, which requires a new Messenger ("I am reincarnated") to help steer society back to justice:

> ...whenever righteousness is on the decline, unrighteousness is in the ascendant, then I am reincarnated. For the protection of the virtuous, for the extirpation of the evil-doers, and for establishing Dharma [righteousness] on a firm footing, I am born from age to age.[252]

Other Beliefs

Indigenous cultures often share concepts of justice closely intertwined with their relationships to the environment, ancestors and community. These concepts often emphasize balance, reciprocity, and the interconnectedness of all living beings, which all contribute to a holistic understanding of justice.

The ancient Greeks explored the nature of justice through the works of philosophers like Plato and Aristotle. In Plato's *Republic*, the great thinker investigated justice in both the individual and the ideal state, proposing a tripartite division of the soul mirroring the three existing classes of society. Aristotle's *Nicomachean Ethics* explored a kind of distributive justice in which individuals would receive benefits or burdens in proportion to their merits.

As societies advance and revise the meaning and description of justice, it will change to meet the needs of the people of the time. For example, in the US in 1800, there were only a handful of wealthy

---

252 *Bhagavad Gita*, Chapter 4: 7-8.

people. In 2023, 1 percent of the US population owned 89 percent of the country's wealth. Most revolutions have been undertaken for the sake of justice and iniquity.

No matter what one's interpretation of justice, the concept consistently represents pursuit of a more equitable society in which there is fair treatment for each member of humanity.

The Central Principle

It should be no surprise that our most recent wisdom tradition continues to cite justice as a central principle.

> No light can compare with the light of justice. The establishment of order in the world and the tranquillity of the nations depend upon it.[253]

While the concept of justice goes back thousands of years, the concept of *social justice* only recently emerged and in contemporary discourse is understood in different ways. Some believe this evolved concept should focus on how the basic structures of society fairly distribute power, resources and opportunities to various social groups. Others, however, want social justice to focus more on how political and legal decision-making procedures can be made fairer. Still others believe social justice should emphasize repairing major historical injustices; overcoming harmful stigmas and prejudices; and establishing more equitable environmental conditions for everyone. Since these are all valid but competing concerns, is it possible to develop a universal aspiration that motivates all the distinct movements for social justice?

The latest wisdom tradition unequivocally states that humans, as spiritual beings, have a two-fold moral purpose—to develop their latent spiritual and intellectual potentialities and to nurture the well-being and development of a global society. Specific developmental

---

253 Bahá'u'lláh. *Epistle to the Son of the Wolf*, www.bahai.org/r/463236506.

efforts align with the diverse contemporary goals of social justice described above, but the universal aspiration that can bind them all together might be stated this way:

> Social justice is a set of conditions that enables every individual and social group to develop their latent capacities so each can contribute to the flourishing of the entire global society.

Assuming this statement adequately orients us toward a common horizon toward which we can all advance, another question still looms—how can we advance?

Contemporary Methods of Advancing Social Justice

Humanity has experimented with evolving ways of bringing about social justice. Most of them still exist today in a rich stew of distinct movements and methods that sometimes complement each other and occasionally collide in competition.

Violent Insurrections

Some social movements have used violent insurrections to overthrow the status quo and force social or political change. The latest wisdom tradition, however, explicitly forbids politically motivated violence. Protests based on violence are counterproductive, disunifying and often cause the kind of social injustice they seek to overcome as innocent bystanders and uninvolved properties are injured.

Peaceful Protests

Our most recent wisdom tradition accepts the use of peaceful protests against social injustice with a few sensible stipulations.

> Not surprisingly, the recourse of many well-intentioned people faced with the frustration of their efforts is to engage in various forms of public protest. Where reaction of this kind is motivated by the dictates of con-

> science, as opposed to such reasons as the mere venting of personal frustration or violence for its own sake, the results are often extremely positive, contributing in no small measure to the awakening of popular concern and to the required revision of public policy. Obviously, the effectiveness of such intervention depends on the extent to which the 'conscience' motivating the activity is itself enlightened and its dictates relevant to the situation.[254]

Recognizing that all guidance is subject to misinterpretation and requires rational thinking to apply successfully, this wisdom tradition cautions that…

> Conscience… can serve either as a bulwark of an upright character or can represent an accumulation of prejudices learned from one's forebears or absorbed from a limited social code.[255]

In other words, to peacefully protest integration in schools based on a conscience contaminated with racist prejudice would be wrong in light of this wisdom tradition's principle of humanity's essential oneness.

Electoral Politics

Social justice is often pursued through conventional mechanisms of the state such as the passing of laws or regulations, taxation, and official social programs. Because our latest wisdom tradition advises against activities that cause disunity, it would be paradoxical for it to support partisan efforts to affect social change. By definition, partisan politics is disunifying. While this recent wisdom tradition

---

[254] "The Bahá'í Faith and Politics: A compilation of Bahá'í texts," Bahais of the United States, Office of Public Affairs.

[255] "The Bahá'í Faith and Politics: A compilation of Bahá'í texts," Bahais of the United States, Office of Public Affairs.

encourages individuals to freely vote their conscience in all elections, its followers do not participate in caucuses or vote in primary elections that require identification with one party or another.

> What we... must face is the fact that society is disintegrating so rapidly that moral issues which were clear a half century ago are now hopelessly confused and what is more, thoroughly mixed up with battling political interests...[256]

In this view, partisanship of any kind works to prevent the unity of humanity. Since partisanship is inherently polarizing, it fundamentally works against unity. Many people, however, behave as if the opposite were true, perhaps because our upbringings have promoted now-obsolete beliefs such as "love of one's country requires active participation in partisan politics." A new system of enacting healthy social change proposed by our newest wisdom tradition suggests that...

> We must build up our... system, and leave the faulty systems of the world to go their way. We cannot change them through becoming involved in them; on the contrary, they will destroy us.[257]

This book is an attempt to explain the features of that system for social change. For those who complain that political non-involvement may be unpatriotic, this wisdom tradition answers:

> It should be made unmistakably clear that such an attitude implies neither the slightest indifference to the cause and interests of their own country, nor

---

256 Shoghi Effendi, *Directives from the Guardian*, pp. 54-57
257 Letter of the Universal House of Justice, December 8, 1967 (Wellspring of Guidance, pp. 131-136)

> involves any insubordination on their part to the authority of recognized and established governments. Nor does it constitute a repudiation of their sacred obligation to promote, in the most effective manner, the best interests of their government and people. It indicates the desire cherished by every true and loyal follower... to serve, in an unselfish, unostentatious and patriotic fashion, the highest interests of the country to which he belongs, and in a way that would entail no departure from the high standards of integrity and truthfulness...[258]

In a sense, this is a call for all citizens to become super-citizens not by contributing to disunity through partisanship activities but through personal activities. Each person can show their love for country...

> ...by serving its well-being in their daily activity, or by working in the administrative channels of the government instead of through party politics or in diplomatic or political posts.[259]

This proposal for nonparticipation in partisan politics is both supremely democratic and a model of moderation in that its conception of social life...

> ...is essentially based on the subordination of the individual will to that of society. It neither suppresses the individual nor does it exalt him to the point of making him an antisocial creature, a menace to society. As in everything, it follows the "golden mean."[260] The only

---

258 Bahá'u'lláh, *The World Order of Bahá'u'lláh*, pp. 64-67, 199

259 Letter from The Universal House of Justice to National Spiritual Assemblies in Africa, February 8. 1970.

260 The golden mean is an approach to ethics usually ascribed to Aristotle

> way that society can function is for the minority to follow the will of the majority.²⁶¹

Contentious Politics

Beyond the conventional responses to injustice mentioned above, some activists and movements engage in contentious politics ranging from civil disobedience and worker strikes to the destruction of property and acts of terrorism.²⁶² These are attempts to apply external forces of moral, political or economic pressure through collective action.

Nonviolent Resistance

Research on contentious politics has recently begun to focus on strategies of nonviolent resistance. Empirical studies have shown that these strategies are often more successful in achieving meaningful social change than their more contentious or violent alternatives.²⁶³ Due to practical and moral constraints, the effectiveness of nonviolent resistance appears in part to come from the greater ease of mobilizing a significant percentage of the population in a nonviolent movement than to a violent insurrection. Nonviolent protest also appears to attract broader public sympathies in support of a cause.

Nonviolence is a moral and spiritual principle that appeared in Jainism and continued through Buddhism, Christianity and other wisdom traditions. In the nineteenth century, large-scale, organized nonviolent movements began to emerge around the same time that our most recent wisdom tradition, the Bahá'í Faith, originated in

---

that emphasizes finding the appropriate medium or middle ground between extremes.

261 Shoghi Effendi, "Directives from the Guardian," no. 144.

262 See Charles Tilly, *Contentious Performances* (Cambridge: Cambridge University Press, 2008).

263 Erica Chenowith and Maria Stephan, *Why Civil Resistance Works: The Strategic Logic of Nonviolent Conflict* (New York: Columbia University Press, 2011).

Persia and promoted the concept. During the twentieth century, nonviolent resistance and protests were refined and popularized by Mahatma Gandhi in South African and India. Later, these nonviolent strategies were adapted to deal with other twentieth century injustices including the civil rights movement in the US during the 1960s. Even more recently, numerous training centers for nonviolent collective action have sprung up globally.

Of course, some nonviolent tactics such as civil disobedience, while effective in some cases, can undercut a broader rule of law. Our most recent wisdom tradition thus emphasizes that the rule of law is essential to social progress.

> ...in order to establish a better social order and economic condition, there must be allegiance to the laws and principles of government.[264]

Expanding on this theme of obedience, this wisdom tradition stated:

> What [this] statement really means is obedience to a duly constituted government, whatever that government may be in form. We are not the ones... to judge our government as just or unjust—for each believer would be sure to hold a different viewpoint, and within our own... fold a hotbed of dissension would spring up and destroy our unity.[265]

The authors think that the implication in this guidance is for all religions and their clergy to refrain from promoting or criticizing current government officials or policies, as this too can create disunity—"a hotbed of dissension"—within religious organizations and houses of worship. In the twenty-first century, we have seen

---

264 'Abdu'l-Bahá, *The Promulgation of Universal Peace*.
265 Shoghi Effendi, *Directives from the Guardian*, pp. 54-57.

clergy become vocal partisan surrogates for political candidates and churches condemn established government policies. In some Christian churches, registered Democrats and Black Americans are unwelcome—not a charitable attitude as recommended by Jesus. Some synagogues openly condemn the positions of Republican officials while others embrace the same. Surely, this is not a path to greater unity among people.

The language of "resistance" implies a struggle against something. Our latest wisdom tradition transforms this concept by emphasizing the positive impact that can be achieved rather than which forces must be resisted. Its Writings suggest that historical progress toward justice, peace and shared human prosperity accelerates when there is an increase in human capacity to apply spiritual principles—or fundamental truths about human existence—to the development of more mature social forms.

Such constructive efforts are active, not reactive. They create something new, not resist something old. Ironically, such constructive efforts often encounter resistance from those who seek to prevent change. In this sense, the newest wisdom tradition's plan for social change is not simply reacting to or resisting the injustices of the current social order. Instead, achievement of the plan is energized by diverse people attracted to a compelling vision of a more just and peaceful world and inspired to become protagonists in a society-building mission to establish a new social order.

Enforcement of Beliefs

In many countries, including the US, activists with strong religious, moral or political beliefs have attempted to impose those beliefs on others, sometimes on *all* members of their society. Suggestions to make the US a "Christian nation" have frequently appeared in public discourse with clear implications for the repression of other faiths. Gender fluidity and identity has become a subject of fierce political conflict; laws have been proposed in many jurisdictions to suppress the rights of LGTBQIA individuals based primarily on the moral views of the proponents. Many people who strongly oppose abortion seek to curb women's reproduction rights despite fierce disagreement from others, in many cases the majority.

Our newest wisdom tradition teaches that no individual or organization should impose their beliefs or practices on others. They believe the patterns of community life they are constructing, along with the administrative structures that support those patterns, will only be viable if they are embraced through a supremely voluntary process. In this regard, Bahá'ís reject all forms of force, coercion, compulsion, pressure, or proselytization as means of social change. The seriousness of this guidance is highlighted in a Message to the followers of the Bahá'í Faith, the most recent wisdom tradition, about causing individuals to accept its Teachings.

> Only if people voluntarily accept them and submit themselves freely to this Order will it be implemented in the world. Bahá'ís should never attempt to impose their belief on anyone... they offer these teachings to the rest of mankind. Whosoever accepts them is a Bahá'í, but everyone is free to reject them. No one is ever compelled to become a Bahá'í, nor is anyone compelled to remain a Bahá'í. If one has accepted the Bahá'í Faith and later concludes that one has made a mistake, one is free to withdraw, and no stigma is attached to such an action.[266]

The strategy proposed by this latest wisdom tradition is consistently one of strategy and attraction: "Construct a viable alternative to prevailing social norms and structures and, to the extent it proves itself more just and inclusive, it will steadily attract

---

266 Universal House of Justice, "Messages from the Universal House of Justice: 1986-2001." Available at https://bahai-library.com/link/6B2nC/uhj_messages_1986_2001.

more and more people. When Bahá'ís encounter repression in this process, they adopt a posture of resilience while laboring on with their constructive efforts."[267]

Collective Learning about Collective Action

Divine guidance is not static, and human learning is always incomplete. Societies must learn to be better at discerning the lessons that our collective life on this planet teaches us. We must learn to recognize those feeble attempts to achieve social justice that clearly do not work, and we must learn to acknowledge what efforts are successful and put them to work more broadly.

Social change is not a project undertaken by one group to help another. It is a team effort. How much better if the appropriate collective action based on our most advanced learning is undertaken by a team comprised of a united global humanity.

> Justice demands universal participation. Thus, while social action may involve the provision of goods and services in some form, its primary concern must be to build capacity within a given population to participate in creating a better world.[268]

---

[267] Michael Karlberg, "The Pursuit of Social Justice," August 3, 2022. Available at: https://bahaiworld.bahai.org/library/the-pursuit-of-social-justice/.

[268] Universal House of Justice, "The Five Year Plan: 2011-2016: Messages of the Universal House of Justice."

Chapter 11:
Human Rights

A Product of Modernity

Ironically, religion and the concept of human rights have long been in substantial conflict. One might expect them to be in accord since the world's wisdom traditions promote key human values such as respect and love for all people. And yet, scholars have determined that before 1400 AD, no known language even contained a word or phrase for the concept of human rights. Certainly, this unnamed issue existed in earlier times, but it remained unrecognized or unaddressed until recently.

Between the thirteenth century BC and the seventh century AD, religious texts appeared in agrarian societies that granted few private rights and even fewer public ones to individuals,[269] so the people for whom these Scriptures were intended probably would not have understood the concept of human rights. As religious groups and communities developed, they often faced difficulties with the

---

[269] Hans Küng and Jürgen Moltmann, *The Ethics of World Religions and Human Rights*; Benjamin Constant, "The Liberty of the Ancients Compared with that of the Moderns," in Diane Ravitch and Abigail Thernstron, eds., *The Democracy Reader*.

modern notions of rights to privacy and free speech precisely because private ethical behavior and public conformance to doctrine often defines the social group.

In 1789, the first nations to adopt formal definitions of human rights—the United States with its Bill of Rights and France with its Declaration of the Rights of Man and of the Citizen—limited those rights to White, property-owning males. This was the tenuous beginning of the Enlightenment, also called the Age of Reason, a period of rigorous scientific, political and philosophical discourse that flourished in European society until the end of the Napoleonic Wars in 1815.

Then, in the nineteenth century, Roman Catholic popes and Muslim clergy all railed against certain rights encouraged by Enlightenment thinkers. Some of this religious opposition to human rights predictably arose from the concept's association with political "liberalism," which had been a significant force in its development and in opposing oppressive ideologies such as fascism, communism and antiliberalism. Prior to World War II, in stark contrast to political liberalism, Roman Catholics in France and other countries were mostly aligned with the political Right, which in Europe considered the ideals of the Enlightenment and the French Revolution with great suspicion. Muslim authorities likewise rejected liberalism, democracy and human rights as anathema, and many do to this day.

The first truly egalitarian, global human rights document originated with the United Nations in 1948—The Universal Declaration of Human Rights (UDHR). It is today the basis for international law and has become the most widely translated document in history.

As we pointed out earlier, however, almost a century before the UN promulgated its UDHR, the Bahá'í Faith—our most recent wisdom tradition—became the first world religion to call unequivocally for universal rights.

> The earth is but one country, and mankind its citizens.[270]

More specifically, this new wisdom tradition taught that…

> …an equal standard of human rights must be recognized and adopted. In the estimation of God all men are equal; there is no distinction or preferment for any soul in the dominion of His justice and equity.[271]

In a presentation made to the first session of the UN Commission on Human Rights in 1947, our most recent wisdom tradition, under the banner of the Bahá'í International Community, stated:

> The whole conception of right has undergone change. A right formerly was a defense against an invasion; a right today is a sharing of social status among mankind. Moral and social law can for the first time in human experience blend and unify when humanity as a whole becomes subject to the same law. Everything universal is divine truth; everything limited and partisan is human opinion.[272]

From John Locke through Thomas Jefferson, early modern civil rights thinkers usually saw personal rights as deriving from a person's status. Consequently, rights pertained mainly to White, male property-owners. The suggestion that a person could have rights simply because they were human rather than by virtue of property ownership or citizenship or another qualifying status was a new concept in world history.

---

270 Bahá'u'lláh, *Gleanings from the Writings of Bahá'u'lláh*.
271 'Abdu'l-Bahá, *The Promulgation of Universal Peace*, p. 181.
272 "A Baha'i Declaration of Human Obligations and Rights," presented to the first session of the United Nations Commission on Human Rights, 1 February 1947

During the UN's formulation of the UCHR, the Bahá'í Faith was a recognized Non-Governmental Organization (NGO) and submitted position papers on its provisions. The Declaration has been endorsed as contributing to world peace by the Baha'i Universal House of Justice, the Faith's worldwide governing body. When it was introduced in 1948, forty-eight member nations voted for it and eight abstained. One hundred nations who joined the UN later have endorsed the document, though some on a pro forma basis. The sole abstainer was Saudi Arabia, which rejected the Declaration's commitment to freedom of religion.

Considering the silence of previous religious texts on this topic, it is stunning to consider the details and nuances of this recent wisdom tradition's guidance about human rights and its depth of commitment to the cause. Its early and radical advocacy raised a truly global voice for guaranteed rights for all individuals and emphasized the absurdity of prejudices that gave rights to some but not others.

Partially because of the strong emphasis placed on global human rights by this latest wisdom tradition, many Bahá'ís—particularly those in Iran, Yemen and Egypt—have suffered tremendous oppression and persecution, including denial of their fundamental human rights. Progressive Bahá'í teachings on issues related to human rights and the essential unity of all religions have led several governments to prevent Bahá'ís from exercising their rights to education, employment, housing, worship and even burial. The government in Iran has imprisoned, tortured and executed Bahá'ís solely for their apolitical religious beliefs. As we write this chapter, hundreds of Bahá'ís are languishing in cramped and cruel Iranian prisons for the "crime" of being a Bahá'í.[273]

Many governments and the UN have relentlessly denounced these disgraceful violations of basic human rights, which certainly rise to the level of crimes against humanity. Bahá'ís believe that when

---

[273] Human Rights Watch, "Iran: Persecution of Bahá'í's in Iran," available at: https://www.hrw.org/news/2024/04/01/iran-persecution-bahais#:

the world accepts and adopts its vision of protecting human rights for everyone, this oppression and persecution will finally end, not just for Bahá'ís but for many other oppressed peoples.

As in many previous wisdom traditions, the Founder of the Bahá'í Faith, Bahá'u'lláh (a Persian title meaning "the Glory of God"), was severely persecuted by the despotic governments of Iran and the Ottoman Empire for starting a "heretical" religion. Early on, He boldly asserted the existence of common human rights in a Tablet, admonishing the monarchs of the world in these powerful words:

> If ye stay not the hand of the oppressor, if ye fail to safeguard the rights of the downtrodden, what right have ye then to vaunt yourselves among men?[274]

In 1852, Bahá'u'lláh was falsely accused of sedition in Tehran and imprisoned in the dreaded Siyah Chal, an infamous dungeon, for four months before being acquitted and exonerated. Because of His influence among the general populace, however, He was eventually exiled and finally incarcerated in the prison-fortress city of Akká (also known as Acre), the Devil's Island of the Ottoman Empire. During decades of incarceration, He was a prisoner of conscience and never convicted of any crime. In 1891, addressing the Qajar state in Iran, he wrote:

> They that perpetrate tyranny in the world have usurped the rights of the peoples and kindreds of the earth and are sedulously pursuing their selfish inclinations.[275]

This latest wisdom tradition teaches that the arc of universal human rights will inevitably bend toward justice.

---

274 Bahá'u'lláh, *Summons of the Lord of Hosts*.
275 Bahá'u'lláh, *Fountain of Wisdom*.

> The wrong in the world continues to exist just because people talk only of their ideals, and do not strive to put them into practice. If actions took the place of words, the world's misery would very soon be changed into comfort. My hope for you is that you will ever avoid tyranny and oppression; that you will work without ceasing till justice reigns in every land...[276]

Rights Shared with the UDHR

While promulgated much earlier than the UN Declaration, the Bahá'í Writings correlate closely to the provisions of the Universal Declaration of Human Rights and in some cases call for individuals to have even more rights. What is perhaps more significant is that the rights identified by this latest wisdom tradition are elevated to the status of spiritual principles that raise up humanity and ascribe divine authority to the concept of universal human rights.

The UDHR begins by affirming that all humans are born free and equal in dignity and rights, are endowed with reason and conscience, and should behave toward each other in a spirit of brotherhood. Its second article affirms that everyone possesses these rights regardless of "race, color, sex, language, religion, political or other opinion, national or social origin, property, birth or other status."

Throughout the earlier pages of this book, you have read passages from our most recent wisdom tradition that clearly confirm these human rights under the banner of the oneness of humanity and explain the reasons—such as ancient traditions and outdated prejudices—why so many people fail to enjoy these rights. Universal human rights stem from the inherent dignity of every human being, and dignity in turn is reconfirmed and supported by upholding those rights.

---

276 'Abdu'l-Bahá, *Paris Talks*, p. 16.

The purpose of this chapter is not to catalog all the human rights upheld, but rather to illustrate with a few examples how this most recent wisdom tradition has introduced a necessary update to the continuing revelation of a divine curriculum[277] for a rapidly advancing and expanding humanity.

Equality of Rights

In previous chapters, we have learned that the most recent wisdom tradition strongly underscored the equality of human rights by condemning all forms of prejudice that could lead to oppression of those rights.

> All are equal in the estimation of God; their rights are one and there is no distinction for any soul; all are protected beneath the justice of God.[278]

As befitting a contemporary revelation of practical guidance, a host of modern human rights have been addressed by the latest wisdom tradition including:

Women's Rights

> In this Revelation... the women go neck and neck with the men. In no movement will they be left behind. Their rights with men are equal in degree. They will enter all the administrative branches of politics. They will attain in all such a degree as will be considered the very highest station of the world of humanity and will take part in all affairs.[279]

---

277 The term "divine curriculum" was coined by author Edward Price and first used in his book *The Divine Curriculum, Volume 1, Divine Design: How God's Plan Is Revealed in the World's Great Religions.*

278 US Bahá'í News Service, "Star of the West: Excerpts #6, June 1919–March 1920."

279 'Abdu'l-Bahá, *Paris Talks.*

Right to Worship One's Choice of Religion

> Since it has been demonstrated that the instinct to worship is universal and has been associated with an infinite number of more or less temporary devotional practices, moral systems and social forms, there is no inherent reason why this instinct may not be reaffirmed in terms of loyalty to mankind and devotion to the cause of world unity on all levels.[280]

Right to Personal Freedom

Slavery and bonded labor are great affronts to the concept of human rights. Slavery, however, is permitted in the central texts of most world religions. Ironically, neither the US Bill of Rights nor the French Declaration of the Rights of Men prohibited slavery because the authors envisaged rights as belonging only to White male property owners.

In 1868, the Founder of our latest wisdom tradition commended the government of Queen Victoria for prohibiting slavery and unequivocally stated:

> It is forbidden you to trade in slaves, be they men or women. It is not for him who is himself a servant to buy another of God's servants, and this has been prohibited in His Holy Table.[281]

Right to Free Thought, Expression and Conscience

In a tablet to Nasiru'd-Din Shah, an oppressor of the new Faith, the Founder of the latest wisdom tradition insisted that the powerful

---

[280] "A Baha'i Declaration of Human Obligations and Rights," presented to the first session of the United Nations Commission on Human Rights, 1 February 1947

[281] Bahá'u'lláh, *The Kitáb-i-Aqdas*.

Persian monarch judge the new religious community based on the same criteria used for others.[282] He pointed out that many other denominations and religions inhabited the land, and the new Faith was but one of them. He called for the monarch to fairly judge all these religions with justice, which would disallow arbitrary declarations of heresy based on thought and expression.[283]

From the beginning, this wisdom tradition deplored religious persecution based on an individual's conscience, which is the right to possess whatever religious or metaphysical views one wishes. The following passage implies the illegitimacy of any coercive attempts to interfere with this right:

> [To insure] freedom of conscience and tranquility of heart and soul is one of the duties and functions of government, and is in all ages the cause of progress in development and ascendency over other lands.[284]

A call for all citizens to be judged by one standard to ensure complete equality concludes with this admonition:

> Interference with creed and faith in every country causes manifest detriment, while justice and equal dealing towards all peoples on the face of the earth are the means whereby progress is effected.[285]

Freedom of religion and religious thought has been a stumbling block for some religions because this right loosens the controls of religious authority and threatens dominance. But the most recent wisdom tradition has liberally upheld this right for all

---

282 Bahá'u'lláh, "Lawhi-i-Sultan," in *Alvah-I Nazilih khitab bi Muluk va Ru'asa-yi Ard* (Tehran: Bahá'í Publishing Trust, 126 B.E.) p. 166.
283 Bahá'u'lláh, "Lawhi-i-Sultan," in *Alvah-I Nazilih khitab bi Muluk*, p. 178.
284 'Abdu'l-Bahá, *A Traveler's Narrative*.
285 'Abdu'l-Bahá, *A Traveler's Narrative*.

people. Comparing freedom of religious thought and belief to the acceptability of differing political views, this wisdom tradition stated:

> Just as in the world of politics there is need for free thought, likewise in the world of religion there should be the right of unrestricted individual belief. Consider what a vast difference exists between modern democracy and the old forms of despotism. Under an autocratic government the opinions of men are not free, and development is stifled, whereas in democracy, because thought and speech are not restricted, the greatest progress is witnessed. It is likewise true in the world of religion. When freedom of conscience, liberty of thought and right of speech prevail— that is to say, when every man according to his own idealization may give expression to his beliefs— development and growth are inevitable.[286]

This candidly stated right of freedom of conscience frankly abolishes the concept of heresy, the underpinning of so much religious persecution and personal suffering. Even the institutions of this worldwide wisdom tradition are commanded not to interfere in the beliefs or conscience of believers or non-believers,[287] an astonishing act of institutional self-discipline supporting the fundamental principle of the independent search for truth.

The essential human right to self-expression and to an independent conscience free of coercion is underscored by another passage affirming that at the core of the new wisdom tradition:

> ...lies the principle of the undoubted right of the individual to self-expression, his freedom to declare his conscience and set forth his views... Let us also bear in

---

286 'Abdu'l-Bahá, *The Promulgation of Universal Peace*.
287 'Abdu'l-Bahá, *Talk in Palo Alto*.

> mind that the keynote of the Cause of God is not dictatorial authority, but humble fellowship, not arbitrary power, but the spirit of frank and loving consultation.[288]

Right to Privacy and Property Ownership

Article 12 of the UN's Universal Declaration of Human Rights guarantees a right to privacy and freedom from attacks on honor and reputation, and Article 17 guarantees the right to own property and protection from being deprived of it. Our newest wisdom tradition, many years before the UDHR was drafted, advocated for:

> ...the free exercise of the individual's rights, and the security of his person and property, his dignity and good name... Whatever is in conflict with these measures has already been proved injurious, in every country, and does not concern one locality more than another.[289]

Among the many principles of this new wisdom tradition that were beginning to take root around the world in the 1920s, perhaps none stoked the enmity of Russian Communists more than the institution of private property.[290]

Workers' Rights

The guarantees of privacy and private property are not absolute. Personal property is different than business property, for which rights must be balanced against workers' rights. The UN's Declaration guarantees each worker social security, certain economic and social rights necessary for "the development of his or her personality," limitations on working hours, a standard of living suitable for well-being, a right to work, equal pay for equal work, lack of workplace discrimination, unemployment compensation and health care.

---

288 Shoghi Effendi, *Bahá'í Administraton*.
289 'Abdu'l-Bahá, *The Secret of Divine Civilization*.
290 Shoghi Effendi, *God Passes By*, pp. 360-361.

Astonishingly, the texts of our most recent wisdom tradition also recognize workers' rights, a feature never seen before in religious Scriptures but clearly necessary in the modern world. This wisdom tradition states that, in some cases, governmental and court interventions are justified to resolve and arbitrate labor disputes because such disputes are not purely private but may affect the entire public. It also maintains that society has a legitimate interest in employing progressive taxation and other just measures to prevent the accumulation of wealth from becoming overly stratified.

> If it be right for a capitalist to possess a large fortune, it is equally just that his workman should have a sufficient means of existence.[291]

Providing not just broad aspirations but also practical detail, this newest wisdom tradition also suggests that there can be great benefit in setting aside a 20 percent ownership stake for employees so they can become part-owners of a company for which they work. Besides an adequate wage, it also proposes "a sufficient pension" for workers upon their retirement.[292]

This wisdom tradition emphasizes that:

> It is the duty of those who are in charge of the organization of society to give every individual the opportunity of acquiring the necessary talent in some kind of profession, and also the means of utilizing such a talent, both for its own sake and for the sake of earning the means of his livelihood.[293]

---

291 'Abdu'l-Bahá, *Paris Talks*.
292 'Abdu'l-Bahá, Paris Talks, p. 153; cf. 'Abdu'l-Bahá, quoted in Badi Shams, *A Bahá'í Perspective on Economics of the Future*, (New Delhi: Bahá'í Publishing Trust, 1989), p. 27
293 Shoghi Effendi, *Directives from the Guardian*.

The relationship between worker and employer, however, is a two-way street.

> Every person must have an occupation, a trade or a craft, so that he may carry other people's burdens, and not himself be a burden to others.[294]

Human Rights Are Now Part of Scripture

It sometimes goes unnoticed that human rights are not merely legal protections (where accepted) or social obligations, but spiritual principles essential for the advancement of civilization. Our latest wisdom tradition has made these universal rights part of Scripture so they cannot be nullified by any human enterprise.

The usefulness of documents such as the UN's Declaration are dependent on the degree to which the rights they describe become binding on member states. But these rights are also dependent on the degree to which they become part of society's human values. The human rights presented by our latest wisdom tradition are part of a visionary and systematic plan for advancing society, a plan in which all the principles support and complement each other and none are expendable.

---

294 'Abdu'l-Bahá, from a Tablet translated from the Persian; quoted in Bahá'u'lláh, 'Abdu'l-Bahá, Shoghi Effendi, *Arts and Crafts*.

Chapter 12:
Universal Peace

What Is Peace?

It is an old joke, that every contestant for the Miss America crown professes the same idealistic goal—to help bring about world peace. The humor comes from the seeming impossibility of such an outrageous aspiration. Yet our most recent wisdom tradition brings the horizon of such a possibility closer to our feet while many cynics believe we are standing at the precipice of our extinction.

There are at least two ways of defining the concept of peace. The negative version defines peace simply as the absence of war and conflict. The positive definition, however, views peace as an objective state of social reality in which shared, harmonious relations foster mutual development and communication among individuals and groups.

The latest wisdom tradition consistently advocates for a unique definition of peace. The Arabic word (isláh) used by the most recent Divine Educator to explain the purpose of His Revelation means both "reform" or "reconstruction and peace-making." In many of His Writings, He combines this word with the concept of development (imár) to provide a comprehensive new vision of society's mission to reform, reconstruct and develop the institutions and structures of the world. Fulfillment of such a vision, of course, would require much more than a simple desire for a successful outcome. It would demand a fundamental transformation of all aspects of human existence. Look at the Table of Contents of this book for an outline of the conditions and issues that must be addressed.

Is Universal Peace Really Possible?

Considering the unimaginable horrors inflicted upon humanity by those who stubbornly cling to old patterns of behavior, it is reasonable to question whether universal peace is possible. The most recent wisdom tradition states that it is not only possible but inevitable. Certainly, there are favorable signs—the creation of the League of Nations, succeeded by a more broadly based United Nations organizations; the gaining of independence of most nations on Earth following the Second World War; the interaction of these fledgling nations with older ones in areas of mutual concern; international undertakings in the fields of science, education, law, economics and culture among previously antagonistic peoples and groups; an unprecedented rise in new international humanitarian organizations; the spread of new movements calling for the cessation of war; the widening spread of ordinary people forming networks of interdependence.

Nevertheless, significant barriers to peace persist. Wars have not ended, and new conflicts continue to erupt. Conspicuous flaws in the world order seem to defy a cure. Society is exhibiting a paradoxical contradiction—on one hand, people around the world say they are longing for peace and harmony, but on the other, they believe human beings are hopelessly selfish, aggressive and incapable of establishing an ordered and peaceful world.

Over a century ago, our most recent wisdom tradition recognized this seemingly intractable condition:

> The winds of despair are, alas, blowing from every direction, and the strife that divides and afflicts the human race is daily increasing. The signs of impending convulsions and chaos can now be discerned, inasmuch as the prevailing order appears to be lamentably defective.[295]

A main purpose of the succession of wisdom traditions has been to provide timely guidance to the peoples of the world, so it is reasonable to expect that our most recent wisdom tradition would offer a plan to help us steer out of the quandary in which we find ourselves. Because of the complexity of the problems, however, and the disunity of our many groups and societies, this solution…

> …calls for no less than the reconstruction and the demilitarization of the whole civilized world— a world organically unified in all the essential aspects of its life, its political machinery, its spiritual aspiration, its trade and finance, its script and language, and yet infinite in the diversity of the national characteristics of its federated units.[296]

In other words, positive thoughts and prayers won't be enough.

A Multi-dimensional and Positive Approach

Our latest wisdom tradition's multi-dimensional and positive approach to world peace, written a century-and-a-half ago, incorporates all the aspects addressed today by various contemporary theories and is explicitly expressed in Bahá'u'lláh's many addresses to individual leaders of the world collected in a book entitled *Summons of the Lord of Hosts*. This correspondence reveals a profound and heartfelt call for universal peace. The most remarkable insight we find, however,

---

295 Bahá'u'lláh, *Fountain of Wisdom*.
296 Shoghi Effendi, *The World Order of Bahá'u'lláh*

is not the clear rejection that future wars are inevitable, but rather the linking of war to a failure to provide collective security for all the nations. The tablets in this collection call for a global approach to peace and the establishment of institutions to provide collective security as an essential means of achieving it.

While this wisdom tradition's concept of democracy is more complex than existing democratic institutions and practices, the Tablets emphatically state that democracy is necessary for achieving peace and identify chief impediments such as social inequality, poverty and the arms race between nations. What emerges is a concept of lasting peace as a structure of interdependent social relations including a culture of peace, democracy, collective security, social justice and other elements.

This newest wisdom tradition often refers to the world as the common home of all peoples and defines human beings as those who dedicate themselves to the service of the entire human race, rejecting the reduction of humans to the level of animals. Humans, we are told, were created not for enmity but for solidarity and cooperation. This requires a new definition of honor, in which true honor derives from serving and loving the entire human race.

> O ye beloved of the Lord! Commit not that which defileth the limpid stream of love or destroyeth the sweet fragrance of friendship. By the righteousness of the Lord! Ye were created to show love one to another and not perversity and rancour. Take pride not in love for yourselves but in love for your fellow-creatures. Glory not in love for your country, but in love for all mankind.[297]

This spiritual definition of humanity is equated with a new definition of freedom as overcoming the expired logic of the struggle for existence. The time has come, we are told, for humans to be...

---

297 Bahá'u'lláh, *Fountain of Wisdom*.

> ...free and emancipated from the captivity of the world of nature; for as long as man is captive to nature he is a ferocious animal, as the struggle for existence is one of the exigencies of the world of nature. This matter of the struggle for existence is the fountain-head of all calamities and is the supreme affliction.[298]

Obviously, a new culture of peace is required for us to reflect this wisdom tradition's definition of human beings. In this new culture, identities are defined in terms of interdependence rather than by contrast or opposition to other people, a definition based upon the concept of unity in diversity.

> O well-beloved ones! The tabernacle of unity hath been raised; regard ye not one another as strangers. Ye are the fruits of one tree, and the leaves of one branch.[299]

Thus, democracy, according to this wisdom tradition, is an organic expression of the collective state of humanity comprised of human beings defined as fundamentally spiritual. But this newest wisdom tradition envisions democracy more as the practice of the art of consultation than a constant war of domination, dehumanization, insult and enmity, which it has become in many countries.

If one were to see human beings as spiritual in nature and no longer struggling for existence like animals, a system of collective security offers a pathway to transcend an armed and animalistic culture of mutual estrangement. While pure communism and pure capitalism both reduce humans to the level of the jungle and eliminate human freedoms, social and economic justice are compatible with a culture of peace, democratic order and collective security. Our latest wisdom tradition calls for an end to the arms race and progress toward economic justice.

---

298 'Abdu'l-Bahá, *Selections from the Writings of 'Abdu'l-Bahá*.
299 Bahá'u'lláh, *Tabernacle of Unity*.

> O kings of the earth! We see you increasing every year your expenditures, and laying the burden thereof on your subjects. This, verily, is wholly and grossly unjust... lay not excessive burdens on your peoples. Do not rob them to rear palaces for yourselves; nay rather choose for them that which ye choose for yourselves.[300]

> Should any one among you take up arms against another, rise ye all against him, for this is naught but manifest justice.[301]

A Plan for Universal Peace

If a workable plan to transform the planet into a world of universal peace were possible, it would begin with a statement of purpose. What would it do, and what would it not do? What constraints would it have? What would be the overall implications?

A plan for establishing universal world peace has been proposed to the world by our newest wisdom tradition. Its statement of purpose follows:

> Let there be no misgivings as to the animating purpose... Far from aiming at the subversion of the existing foundations of society, it seeks to broaden its basis, to remold its institutions in a manner consonant with the needs of an ever-changing world. It can conflict with no legitimate allegiances, nor can it undermine essential loyalties. Its purpose is neither to stifle the flame of a sane and intelligent patriotism in men's hearts, nor to abolish the system of national autonomy so essential if the evils of excessive centralization are

---

300 Bahá'u'lláh, *The Summons of the Lord of Hosts*.
301 Shoghi Effendi, *The World Order of Bahá'u'lláh*.

> to be avoided. It does not ignore, nor does it attempt to suppress, the diversity of ethnical origins, of climate, of history, of language and tradition, of thought and habit, that differentiate the peoples and nations of the world. It calls for a wider loyalty, for a larger aspiration than any that has animated the human race. It insists upon the subordination of national impulses and interests to the imperative claims of a unified world. It repudiates excessive centralization on one hand, and disclaims all attempts at uniformity on the other. Its watchword is unity in diversity.[302]

A World Parliament

In searching for more details in the Tablets written to many leaders of the world, we find this astonishing proposition:

> What else could these weighty words signify if they did not point to the inevitable curtailment of unfettered national sovereignty as an indispensable preliminary to the formation of the future Commonwealth of all the nations of the world? Some form of a world super-state must needs be evolved, in whose favour all the nations of the world will have willingly ceded every claim to make war, certain rights to impose taxation and all rights to maintain armaments, except for purposes of maintaining internal order within their respective dominions. Such a state will have to include within its orbit an International Executive adequate to enforce supreme and unchallengeable authority on every recalcitrant member of the commonwealth; a World Parliament whose members shall be elected by the people in their respective countries and whose election shall

---

302 Bahá'u'lláh, *The World Order of Bahá'u'lláh*.

> be confirmed by their respective governments; and a Supreme Tribunal whose judgement will have a binding effect even in such cases where the parties concerned did not voluntarily agree to submit their case to its consideration.[303]

This "World Parliament," then, would provide the institutional framework to support a system of collective security. It is up to the governments of the world to determine the exact nature and workings of this body, but all nations must participate in the process.

> The time must come when the imperative necessity for the holding of a vast, an all-embracing assemblage of men will be universally realized. The rulers and kings of the earth must needs attend it, and, participating in its deliberations, must consider such ways and means as will lay the foundations of the world's Great Peace amongst men.[304]

It will take great courage and resolution, pure motive and selfless love from all people to achieve this momentous step toward peace. The process required to arouse the necessary volition is outlined in this book, which is merely a summary of the divine guidance we have been offered.

Regarding the proceedings of this world gathering, we have been provided an abundance of guidance, some of which follows:

> They must make the Cause of Peace the object of general consultation, and seek by every means in their power to establish a Union of the nations of the world. They must conclude a binding treaty and establish a covenant, the provisions of which shall be sound, invio-

---

303 Shoghi Effendi, *The World Order of Bahá'u'lláh*.
304 Bahá'u'lláh, *Fountain of Wisdom*.

> lable and definite. They must proclaim it to all the world and obtain for it the sanction of all the human race. This supreme and noble undertaking—the real source of the peace and well-being of all the world—should be regarded as sacred by all that dwell on earth. All the forces of humanity must be mobilized to ensure the stability and permanence of this Most Great Covenant.

> In this all-embracing Pact the limits and frontiers of each and every nation should be clearly fixed, the principles underlying the relations of governments towards one another definitely laid down, and all international agreements and obligations ascertained. In like manner, the size of the armaments of every government should be strictly limited, for if the preparations for war and the military forces of any nation should be allowed to increase, they will arouse the suspicion of others. The fundamental principle underlying this solemn Pact should be so fixed that if any government later violate any one of its provisions, all the governments on earth should arise to reduce it to utter submission, nay the human race as a whole should resolve, with every power at its disposal, to destroy that government. Should this greatest of all remedies be applied to the sick body of the world, it will assuredly recover from its ills and will remain eternally safe and secure.[305]

The authors of this book believe that such an important assembly is long overdue. The forces of history are pushing us toward this act, which will mark the long-awaited dawn of humanity's coming of age. In the meantime, we can work individually to conduct ourselves according to the principles that lead to unbiased love and unity.

---

305 'Abdu'l-Bahá, *The Secret of Divine Civilization*.

A Living Pattern for a Successful Society

Humanity tends to look for prototypes of success. The believers who follow the teachings of our latest wisdom tradition are creating a pattern for a unified global community of millions of people from many nations, cultures, classes and creeds. Increasingly, people from other faiths and no faith at all are participating in this community as a means of increasing their capacity to take charge of their own spiritual, social and intellectual development. Newly found friends engage with enrolled members in:

> ...meetings that strengthen the devotional character of the community; classes that nurture the tender hearts and minds of children; groups that channel the surging energies of junior youth; circles of study, open to all, that enable people of varied backgrounds to advance on equal footing and explore the application of the teachings to their individual lives.[306]

This community represents the great diversity of the human family—a pattern of unity in diversity. The affairs of enrolled members are governed through a system of consultative principles operating under democratically elected international governing councils ordained at local through and international levels by the Founder of the most recent wisdom tradition. This unified collection of diverse peoples seeks to realize the Founder's vision and demonstrate its practicality, helping to unify hearts and minds to bring about an ever-advancing civilization.

---

306 Universal House of Justice, Ridvan 2010 letter.

Chapter 13:
The Environment

> This span of earth is but one homeland and one habitation. It behooveth you to abandon vainglory which causeth alienation and to set your hearts on whatever will ensure harmony.[307]

A Lesson in Interdependence

The natural world in all its glory offers us a profound lesson in interdependence. From the entire biosphere to the smallest microorganism, we witness a demonstration of how dependent each life-form is on many others.

> Reflect upon the inner realities of the universe, the secret wisdoms involved, the enigmas, the inter-relationships, the rules that govern all. For every part of the universe is connected with every other part by ties that are very powerful and admit of no imbalance, nor any slackening whatever.[308]

---

307 Bahá'u'lláh, *Fountain of Wisdom*.
308 'Abdu'l-Bahá, *Selections from the Writings of 'Abdu'l-Bahá*.

Humanity is an intimate part of this greater system and relies on it in numerous ways. But currently, it faces a paradox that has never existed before. On one hand, humankind has never possessed more power to reshape the natural world on a planetary scale, evidence of our collective ingenuity to develop technology to suit our needs and desires. On the other hand, however, when this technological wizardry is unleashed without thoughtful consideration for consequences and is directed by priorities contrary to the common good, this power can be globally destructive and potentially irreversible.

> ...is there any deed in the world that would be nobler than service to the common good?... No, by the Lord God![309]

The passage above, from our most recent wisdom tradition, was written in 1875 during the lifetime of Pope Pius IX. About 140 years later, Pope Francis, in the encyclical letter Laudato Si ("Praised Be"), publicly concurred with this view and echoed many other proclamations of the new wisdom tradition when he wrote:

> The notion of the common good also extends to future generations... We can no longer speak of sustainable development apart from intergenerational solidarity. Once we start to think about the kind of world we are leaving to future generations, we look at things differently; we realize that the world is a gift which we have freely received and must share with others. Since the world has been given to us, we can no longer view reality in a purely utilitarian way, in which efficiency and productivity are entirely geared to our individual benefit. Intergenerational solidarity is not optional, but rather a basic question of justice, since the world we have received also belongs to those who will follow us.[310]

---

309 'Abdu'l-Bahá, *The Secret of Divine Civilization*.
310 Pope Francis, the encyclical letter "Laudato Si," (§159)

The Earth has limits that become readily apparent when surpassed. Consider the festering issues of climate change, biodiversity loss, environmental degradation and pollution. The grave effects of injuring and exploiting our planetary home call for collective action, which in turn is based on developing human relationships that are more mature, collaborative and constructive. International advances in addressing scientific, legal and institutional environmental issues over the past half-century offer some optimism. The question before the leaders of the world now is whether essential preventive actions will be taken by rational choice or in response to destruction and suffering in the wake of an escalating environmental breakdown.

Trustees of the Natural World

Of all the forms of life on Earth, humans have unique influence on the natural world. Some people have taken this influence to mean that humans are justified in claiming ownership of land and controlling how it is used. As more people recognize humanity's interdependence on the environment, however, they have begun to accept that with this influence comes great responsibility to nurture and protect the natural world.

> Each of us enters the world as a trust of the whole. Each in turn bears a measure of responsibility for the welfare of all and for the planet on which we depend.[311]

Imminent Perils with Devastating Impacts

Failure to be good trustees of the environment threatens our very existence. Human values and universal peace will mean nothing if our home, planet Earth, can no longer support humanity. The

---

311 "One Planet, One Habitation: A Baha'i Perspective on Recasting Humanity's Relationship with the Natural World." 1 Jun 2022. Available at https://www.bic.org/publications/one-planet-one-habitation.

threats to our survival are brutal and numerous. Air pollution caused by various gases and poisons discharged by industry and farms and the burning of fossil fuels is threatening our health. Water pollution and shortages are turning clean drinking water into an uncommon commodity and starving our agricultural lands of precious moisture. Climate change and global warning are driving to extinction many species, causing mass migrations of life-forms and causing extreme weather events including coastal flooding and massive forest fires.

Disastrous results from around the world are being seen from deforestation, habitat destruction and loss of biodiversity and endangered species; ozone layer depletion; surfacing of toxic chemicals and emissions from mining; natural disasters, many caused by human actions; accidental or purposeful release of nuclear waste; light and noise pollution in urban areas; the sprawl of urban residential areas and landfills.

The task of building a sustainable and flourishing world holds the promise of providing a point of unity not only in shared endeavor but in joyful celebration. In return, the unity expanded by such a collaborative undertaking can magnify the results exponentially.

Nature is an Emanation of God's Will

Our latest wisdom tradition links our trusteeship of the Earth's ecosystem with humanity's spiritual nature by identifying three underlying principles.

- The oneness of humanity is the fundamental spiritual and social truth shaping our age.
- All material things are interconnected and flourish according to the law of reciprocity (mutual benefit.)
- Nature reflects the qualities and attributes of God, therefore nature should be greatly respected and cherished.

> Nature in its essence is the embodiment of My Name, the Maker, the Creator. His manifestations are diversified by varying causes, and in this diversity there are signs for men of discernment. Nature is God's Will and is its expression in and through the contingent world.[312]

Understanding nature as a reflection of the majesty of a Supreme Being and an expression of His purpose inspires astonishment and respect for the world in which we live. It helps us understand that politics, profit and prejudice should be removed from all decisions about how to protect and nurture the environment. The latest wisdom tradition describes nature as an emanation of the Will of God, which removes it from the dominion of humankind and makes of it a bounty and a lesson for us all, as in this prayer:

> ...every time I turn my gaze to Thine earth, I am made to recognize the evidences of Thy power and the tokens of Thy bounty. And when I behold the sea, I find that it speaketh to me of Thy majesty, and of the potency of Thy might, and of Thy sovereignty and Thy grandeur. And at whatever time I contemplate the mountains, I am led to discover the ensigns of Thy victory and the standards of Thine Omnipotence.[313]

To think of the natural world as an emanation of God's Will makes humankind's continuous destruction the environment seem a blasphemy. The texts of our most recent wisdom tradition repeatedly call for deep respect for all the life-forms of the Earth's ecosystem. But seeing the reflection of God's attributes in nature should not be viewed as a call to worship nature. In fact, humankind possesses the capacity to emancipate itself from the world of nature:

---

312 Bahá'u'lláh, *Fountain of Wisdom*.
313 Bahá'u'lláh, *Prayers and Meditations*.

> And among the teachings… is man's freedom, that… he should be free and emancipated from the captivity of the world of nature; for as long as man is captive to nature he is a ferocious animal, as the struggle for existence is one of the exigencies of the world of nature.[314]

Earth's Resources

The coming of age of humanity requires an organic change in the structure of society to reflect the interdependence of all its elements and humanity's reciprocal relationship with the natural world that sustains it. Such a transformation can only come from a wholesale change in the attitudes and behaviors of the world's citizens.

> The inward life of man as well as his outward environment have to be reshaped if human salvation is to be secured.[315]

In the view of the authors, "the inward life of man" is a reference to his rational soul, which needs to be put into action to solve his environmental issues as well as other issues that confront everyone on a daily bases. Earth's resources, however, will always be needed to sustain humanity, which is…

> …constantly taking out of nature's laboratory new and wonderful things.[316]

Too often, though, humankind exhausts the soil through destructive farming practices, pollutes the waterways with waste and toxic chemicals, voraciously strip mines for precious metals, and deforests millions of acres, leaving behind ecological devastation.

---

314 'Abdu'l-Bahá, *Selections from the Writings of 'Abdu'l-Bahá*.
315 Letter written on behalf of Shoghi Effendi to an individual believer, 27 May 1932.
316 'Abdu'l-Bahá, *The Promulgation of Universal Peace*.

During this tempestuous time, humanity's actions are not yet influenced by wisdom and maturity. The current world order has failed to protect the environment from its trustees. Consciousness of the oneness of humankind fosters a recognition that the earth's wealth and wonders are the common heritage of all people and they deserve equitable access to these resources.

Society continues to prize expansion, acquisition, creation of wealth and gratification of wants. These selfish goals are not by themselves realistic guides to policy. On the other hand, neither is the romantic deification nature sufficient to ward off imminent disaster.

Since humanity depends on Earth's resources, the pressing issues for today are practical ones—how to best use the land and develop technology that serves the community appropriately, and how to produce and distribute goods and services to people equitably.

Policies and structures arising from partisan politics have been unable to adequately address these basic issues, promote meaningful respect for the earth, or responsibly organize and fully utilize its raw materials. Our most recent wisdom tradition envisions that one positive outcome of the unification of humankind will be the emergence of a federated, integrated system of global governance capable of coordinating an equitable distribution of Earth's resources and providing legal protections for universal well-being.[317]

Animals

Being stewards of the natural world rationally extends to caring for the animal realm.

> Train your children from their earliest days to be infinitely tender and loving to animals. If an animal be sick, let the children try to heal it, if it be hungry, let them feed it, if thirsty, let them quench its thirst, if weary, let them see that it rests.[318]

---

317 Shoghi Effendi, *The World Order of Bahá'u'lláh*.
318 'Abdu'l-Bahá, *Selections from the Writings of 'Abdu'l-Bahá*.

As a practical measure, however, this wisdom tradition recognizes that some animals can behave dangerously, and so it makes necessary exceptions for...

> ...animals which are harmful... such as poisonous snakes, and similar pernicious creatures, the reason being that kindness to these is an injustice to human beings and to other animals as well.[319]

Even in a natural world of adversaries and opposing forces, we can see the interconnectedness of all created things.

> Were one to observe with an eye that discovereth the realities of all things, it would become clear that the greatest relationship that bindeth the world of being together lieth in the range of created things themselves, and that co-operation, mutual aid and reciprocity are essential characteristics in the unified body of the world of being, inasmuch as all created things are closely related together and each is influenced by the other or deriveth benefit therefrom, either directly or indirectly.[320]

Biodiversity

The virtues of human diversity highlighted in the texts of our newest wisdom tradition apply equally to the concept of biodiversity when it states:

> ...diversity is the essence of perfection and the cause of the appearance of the bestowals of the Most Glorious Lord. This diversity, this difference is like the naturally created dissimilarity and variety of the limbs and

---

[319] 'Abdu'l-Bahá, *Selections from the Writings of 'Abdu'l-Bahá.*
[320] 'Abdu'l-Bahá, "Social and Economic Development."

> organs of the human body, for each one contributed to the beauty, efficiency and perfection of the whole...[321]

Biodiversity, then, is a required condition of an ecosystem.

> Know that the order and perfection of the universe require that existence should appear in countless forms. Created things cannot therefore be realized in a single degree, station, manner, kind, or species: Differences of degree, distinctions in form, and a multiplicity of kinds and species are inevitable.[322]

Transformation of Views about the Natural World

In general, the views of humanity about the value of the natural world and humanity's stewardship of it must be transformed if a sustainable environment is to continue. This transformation can be assisted by the passing of relevant laws and regulations, but this will never be enough to save us from ourselves, because the spiritual and material planes of existence are interconnected and act upon each other.

> We cannot segregate the human heart from the environment outside us and say that once one of these is reformed everything will be improved. Man is organic with the world. His inner life molds the environment and is itself also deeply affected by it. The one acts upon the other and every abiding change in the life of man is the result of these mutual reactions.[323]

In the view of our most recent wisdom tradition, the natural world is so utterly interconnected to humanity and everything else

---

321 'Abdu'l-Bahá, "Tablets to the Hague."
322 'Abdu'l-Bahá, *Some Answered Questions*.
323 Shoghi Effendi, quoted in *Compilations, The Compilation of Compilations*, vol I, p. 84.

that only a universal acceptance and adherence to the principle of the oneness of humanity can have a direct and enduring impact on our spiritual, social and physical environments. Acceptance of this principle will ultimately entail a major restructuring of the world's educational, social, agricultural, industrial, economic, legal and political systems. Out of this restructuring will emerge a sustainable, just and prosperous world civilization.

Our environmental issues cannot be solved alone because they are interconnected with everything else. Ultimately, only a unified civilization…

> …in which science and religion work in harmony will be able to restore and preserve ecological balance, foster stability in our human population and advance both the material and spiritual well-being of all peoples and nations.[324]

Redefining Progress and Development

Refashioning humanity's relationship with the natural world will require redefining our notions of progress, civilization and development. Consider the topic of budgets. In some quarters, budgets for environmental investment or development efforts are intelligently being tied to indicators of progress that are more holistic than gross domestic product (GDP) to address other issues such as well-being. More expansion of this viewpoint is needed to explore fundamental issues such as: What are the qualities by which a person, nation or organization is judged as successful? For which attributes are they commended and appreciated?

If the answers to such questions value possessions over relationships or acquisitions over responsible actions, a sustainable

---

324 "Bahá'í Faith Statement on the Environment," issued by the Bahá'í Office of the Environment on behalf of the Bahá'í International Community; available at: https://interfaithsustain.com/bahai-faith-statement-on-the-environment/.

world will remain out of reach. Prioritizing material values by their very nature urges humanity to excess, exploitation, and inevitably to depletion of resources once prized. They also foster the gross extremes of isolated wealth and debilitating poverty. Only when these counterproductive materialistic values are set aside can we resolve their profound contradictions, among them the expectation of infinite growth on a finite planet. Only when progress is understood in new terms can the main drivers of our environmental crisis be correctly identified so lasting change can be made.

No country has mastered the process of sustainable development, though some forms of new technological capacity, industrialization and economic growth have been referred to as successful development efforts. True sustainable development, however, remains elusive judging from the dissatisfaction of multitudes stuck in areas traditionally thought of as developed. The injustices inflicted upon countless others, and the pressures currently stressing the natural world, demonstrate that our current definition of development is incomplete at best and too often damaging.

> As trustees, or stewards, of the planet's vast resources and biological diversity, humanity must learn to make use of the earth's natural resources, both renewable and non-renewable, in a manner that ensures sustainability and equity into the distant reaches of time. This attitude of stewardship will require full consideration of the potential environmental consequences of all development activities. It will compel humanity to temper its actions with moderation and humility, realizing that the true value of nature cannot be expressed in economic terms… Therefore, sustainable environmental management must come to be seen not as a discretionary commitment mankind can weigh against other competing interests, but rather as a fundamental responsibility that

> must be shouldered—a pre-requisite for spiritual development as well as the individual's physical survival.[325]

Earth, its diverse peoples and other creatures have suffered from a materialistic concept of the individual as a purely self-interested economic unit competing with all others to accumulate an increasing share of the world's limited material resources. "This caricature has been largely rejected... as simplistic and crude. Many aspects of the global order still rest on these assumptions, however, and often reinforce and deepen them."[326]

> The faculties needed to construct a more just and sustainable social order—moderation, justice, love, reason, sacrifice and service to the common good—have too often been dismissed as naïve ideals. Yet, it is these, and related, qualities that must be harnessed to overcome the traits of ego, greed, apathy and violence, which are often rewarded by the market and political forces driving current patterns of unsustainable consumption and production.[327]

Shattering this paradigm and advancing the concept of the oneness of humanity can open minds to a profoundly different and more optimistic reality that can rebuild humanity's relationship with the natural world.

---

325 Bahá'í International Community, "Valuing Spirituality in Development: Initial Considerations Regarding the Creation of Spiritually Based Indicators for Development." A concept paper written for the World Faiths and Development Dialogue, Lambeth Palace, London, 18-19 February 1998.

326 "One Planet, One Habitation: A Bahá'í Perspective on Recasting Humanity's Relationship with the Natural World," Stockholm, 1 June 2022. Available at: https://www.bic.org/statements/one-planet-one-habitation-bahai-perspective-recasting-humanitys-relationship-natural-world.

327 Bahá'í International Community, "Rethinking Prosperity: Forging Alternatives to a Culture of Consumerism," 2010.

Chapter 14:
The Prosperity of Humankind

In this concluding chapter, the authors have attempted to pull together the many threads of a systematic plan for developing an ever-advancing society, the main elements of which are chapters in this book. Our latest wisdom tradition has offered this optimistic plan to the world, and we hope to show how and why the various elements of the plan are necessary. The goal of this plan is the prosperity of humankind physically, emotionally, spiritually, and rationally, with all humanity equitably enjoying peace and freedom. This final chapter includes updated and adapted content from "The Prosperity of Humankind," a statement prepared by the Bahá'í International Community Office of Public Affairs, Haifa.[328]

A Vision of Prosperity for All Humankind

Throughout the world, people are yearning for an end to conflict and suffering and ruin. These impulses for change must be channeled to overcome the barriers that block fulfillment of the long-awaited

---

[328] "The Prosperity of Humankind," A statement prepared by the Bahá'í International Community Office of Public Affairs, Haifa. Available online at: https://www.bahai.org/library/other-literature/official-statements-commentaries/prosperity-humankind/1#652797715.

promise of peace for our planet. This enormous task will require a massive effort that cannot be rallied merely by making the usual public appeals. It can only be motivated by a vision of human prosperity in the fullest sense, and the beneficiaries of this prosperity must be all inhabitants of the planet without distinction or conditions. The authors suggest that the time has come for all humanity to direct their affairs—religious, political, personal, and social—in a rational manner so that all decisions made will apply equally to everyone and stand the test of time. This emotional commitment to ignorance has to stop if we wish to live to see an ever advancing civilization.

In the past century, we have witnessed unification of the world physically and economically because of high-speed communications and travel. We have come to experience the interdependence of all who live on it. Endowed with a wealth of genetic and cultural diversity, the world's inhabitants are now being challenged to draw on their shared inheritance to assume the responsibility for designing their own future.

An advancement of civilization cannot be possible, however, without reexamining the attitudes and assumptions that underlie social and economic development. As this rethinking process unfolds, fundamental issues are emerging related to long-term goals, future social structures, principles of social justice and the role of knowledge in affecting change.

In virtually all societies, the primary purpose of current social and economic development is to achieve the kinds of material prosperity that characterize the most developed regions of the world. The development planning processes may accommodate cultural and political differences and respond to the dangers of environmental degradation, but the basic materialistic goals of development have always stubbornly resisted challenge. It is no longer possible to believe that this stalled approach to social and economic development will continue to meet humanity's expanding needs without widening the gulf between the wealthy, who can purchase whatever they want, and the escalating population of poverty-stricken inhabitants, who struggle for survival.

Redefining the Purpose of Development

The unprecedented crisis of economic disparity has in part helped spawn a social breakdown that highlights a profound conceptual error about human nature itself. The response of human beings to this crisis demonstrates that the incentives of the prevailing order are not only inadequate but seem almost irrelevant in the face of world events. Until development efforts find a purpose beyond mere economic reward, they will fail even to attain their basic material goals. That purpose must be pursued in the motivating spiritual dimensions of life that rise above economic incentives and transcend an artificially imposed division of societies into "developed" and "developing."

The crucial role of government in development efforts requires no elaboration. It is almost incomprehensible, however, that even in democracies, the masses of humanity are seen by leaders and planners as recipients of benefits from aid and training and not as full participants in the formation of these efforts. Planners acknowledge public participation as a principle, but the public's role in decision-making is at best limited to a narrow range of choices pre-selected by inaccessible agencies and determined by goals that citizens cannot reconcile with their perceptions of reality.

This patriarchal approach is endorsed—implicitly if not explicitly—by established religions that are encumbered by traditions of paternalism. Prevalent religious thought seems incapable of transforming a person's belief in the spiritual dimensions of human nature into confidence in humanity's collective capacity to surpass material conditions.

Movements of Change

If it is true that the world's governments are striving through the United Nations system to construct a new global order, it is perhaps equally true that the world's inhabitants are galvanized by this same vision. The global response has produced a sudden flowering of countless movements and organizations of social change at local, regional and international levels. Human rights, the advance of women, the social requirements of sustainable economic development, the overcoming of prejudices, the moral education of children, the promotion of universal education and a host of other vital concerns each commands urgent advocacy. As demonstrated throughout this book, these issues are each addressed as part of a cohesive system offered by the latest wisdom tradition.

> Be anxiously concerned with the needs of the age ye live in, and centre your deliberations on its exigencies and requirements.[329]

The Oneness of Humanity

Recognition of the oneness of humankind is the bedrock of a strategy that can motivate the world's population to take responsibility for its collective destiny. Deceptively simple, the concept that all humanity is comprised of a single people presents difficult challenges to the way most institutions carry out their functions because conflict is today the mainspring of human interaction. This can be seen in the adversarial structure of civil government and the courts, the advocacy principle informing most of civil law, a glorification of struggles between classes and other social groups, even the competitive spirit dominating so much of modern life.

Diversity and Interconnection

The latest wisdom tradition compares the world to the human body, which helps explain the concepts of diversity and interconnection.[330]

---

329 Bahá'u'lláh, *The Proclamation of Bahá'u'lláh*, p. 116.
330 Bahá'u'lláh, *The Kitáb-i-Aqdas: The Most Holy Book*

In this analogy, human society is composed not of a mass of merely differentiated cells but of associations of individuals, each of whom is endowed with intelligence and will. The biological form illustrates fundamental principles of existence, chief among which is unity in diversity.

Paradoxically, it is the wholeness and complexity of the human body—and the perfect integration of the body's cells into it—that enable the distinctive capacities of each component to be fully realized. No cell lives apart from the body and all cells contribute to its functioning or share from the well-being of the whole. In turn, the well-being of the body finds its purpose in the expression of human consciousness. In other words, the purpose of biological development is greater than the mere existence of the body and its parts.

What is true of the individual has its parallels in human society. The human species is an organic whole, the leading edge of the evolutionary process. The collective consciousness of humans operates through an infinite diversity of individual minds and motivations. This in no way, however, detracts from its essential unity. In fact, this inherent diversity distinguishes unity from homogeneity or uniformity. The peoples of the world are today experiencing their collective coming-of-age. Because of this emerging maturity, the principles of unity in diversity and interconnection are finally finding their full expression. The process of social organization has successively moved from simple structures of clan and tribe, through countless forms of urban society, to the emergence of the nation-state. Each stage has released a wealth of new opportunities for the application of human capacities.

Universal Laws and Institutions

Laying the groundwork for global civilization calls for the creation of laws and institutions that are universal in character and authority. This effort can begin only when the concept of the oneness of humanity has been wholeheartedly embraced by the lawmakers and organization creators, and when the related principles—described in this book—are adequately propagated. Achieving these milestones starts a process through which humanity can be drawn into establishing common goals and committing to their attainment.

> The well-being of mankind, its peace and security, are unattainable unless and until its unity is firmly established.[331]

The principle of justice can transform the dawning recognition of humanity's oneness into a collective will through which the structures of global community life can be confidently erected. A world that prizes all individuals having access to a diversity of ideas and to information of every kind will find justice becoming the ruling principle of successful social organization.

Justice

For individuals, justice is a faculty of the human soul that enables one to distinguish truth from falsehood. Our latest wisdom tradition confirms that in the sight of God, justice is "the best beloved of all things"[332] since it allows individuals to see with their own eyes rather than the eyes of others. Justice calls for fair-minded judgments and equity in one's treatment of others.

For groups, justice is an indispensable compass in collective decision-making, the only means by which unity of thought and action can be achieved. Far from encouraging a punitive spirit, justice is the practical expression of awareness that the interests of the individual and those of society are indivisibly linked. When it becomes a guiding concern of human interaction, justice permits options to be examined dispassionately and encourages appropriate

---

331 Bahá'u'lláh, *Gleanings from the Writings of Bahá'u'lláh*.
332 Bahá'u'lláh, *The Hidden Words of Bahá'u'lláh*.

courses of action. When a climate of justice prevails, manipulation and partisanship are less likely to influence decisions.

In the task of defining progress, concern for justice helps diminish the temptation to sacrifice the well-being of humankind—and even of the planet itself—to the advantage of privileged minorities. In design and planning, it prevents limited resources from being diverted to projects that do not match a community's priorities. Only development programs perceived as just and equitable can hope to engage the commitment of the masses of humanity.

Human Rights

A successful strategy of social and economic development calls for human rights to be freed from the grip of false dichotomies that have for so long held it hostage. The conviction that every individual should enjoy freedom of thought and action consistent with personal growth does not justify devotion to the cult of individualism that so deeply corrupts contemporary life. Nor does concern to ensure the welfare of society require deification of the state as the supposed source of humanity's well-being.

The history of the previous century clearly demonstrates that such ideologies and the partisan agendas they prop up have been the principal enemies of the very interests they purport to serve. Only in a consultative framework enabled by recognition of humanity's essential unity can the fullest concern for human rights find creative expression.

The term "human rights" came into general use only after the promulgation of the United Nations Charter in 1945 and the adoption of the Universal Declaration of Human Rights three years later. The Declaration passed without a dissenting vote in the General Assembly, conferring on it an authority that has grown steadily.

The freedom to investigate the purpose of existence and make it personally achievable is a distinguishing impulse of human consciousness on which many of the rights enshrined in the Declaration are based on. Universal education, freedom of movement, access to information, and the opportunity to participate in political life are all aspects of it that require explicit protection by the international community. The same is true of freedom of thought and belief, including religious liberty and the right to hold and express opinions.

Since the body of humankind is one and indivisible, each member of the race is born into the world as a trust of the whole. This trusteeship constitutes the moral foundation of most of the other human rights that the instruments of the United Nations have attempted to define. The security of the family and the home, the ownership of property, and the right to privacy are all implied in such a trusteeship.

The principle of collective trusteeship creates the right of all people to expect that those cultural conditions essential to their identities will enjoy legal protection. Like the role played by the gene pool in biological life, the wealth of cultural diversity achieved over thousands of years is vital to the development of a human race experiencing its collective coming of age. This diversity is a heritage that must be honored in a global civilization. On one hand, cultural expressions need to be protected from suffocation by materialistic influences. On the other, cultures must be encouraged to interact with one another in ever-changing patterns of civilization, free of manipulation for partisan ends.

> The light of men is Justice. Quench it not with the contrary winds of oppression and tyranny. The purpose of justice is the appearance of unity among men. The ocean of divine wisdom surgeth within this exalted word, while the books of the world cannot contain its inner significance.[333]

---

333 Bahá'u'lláh, *Fountain of Wisdom*.

Relationships

As the standard of human rights becomes a prevailing international norm, a fundamental redefinition of relationships also becomes necessary. Current conceptions of appropriate relationships—between human beings, between humans and nature, between the individual and society, and between the members of society and its institutions—still reflect an understanding gained during earlier and less mature stages in humanity's development. If humanity is coming of age, if all the inhabitants of the planet constitute a single people, if justice is to be the ruling principle of social organization—then conceptions born out of ignorance of these emerging realities must be recast.

Movement to redefine relationships has barely begun. Eventually, it will lead to a new understanding of the nature of the family and the rights and responsibilities of each member. It will entirely transform the role of women at every level. It will have a sweeping effect in reordering one's relation to work and an understanding of the position occupied by economic activity in their lives. It will change the governance of human affairs and the institutions created to support them. Ultimately, the restructuring or transformation of the United Nations system already underway may lead to the establishment of a world federation of nations with its own legislative, judicial, and executive bodies.

Consultation

Central to reconstituting the system of human relationships is a process our latest wisdom tradition refers to as consultation.

> In all things it is necessary to consult... The maturity of the gift of understanding is made manifest through consultation.[334]

---

334 Bahá'u'lláh, from a Tablet translated from the Persian available at https://www.bahai.org/library/authoritative-texts/compilations/consulta-

The standard for this process of consultation is not the simple pattern of negotiation and compromise that characterizes present-day discussions. It cannot be subject to the culture of protest, another prevailing feature of contemporary society. The purpose of consultation is to arrive at a consensus about the truth of a given situation and the wisest choice of action among the options open at any given moment. The process is undermined by hostile debate, propaganda, the adversarial method, and the entire apparatus of partisanship that has long plagued agreement on collective action.

The latest wisdom tradition calls for a consultative process in which the individual participants strive to rise above their personal points of view to function as members of a unified body with its own interests and goals. In such an atmosphere, characterized by both candor and courtesy, ideas belong not to the individual to whom they occur but to the entire consultative body to consider, discard or revise as democratically decided.

Consultation succeeds to the extent that all participants support the decisions made regardless of the personal opinions or affiliations one held when entering the discussion. If any shortcomings are exposed regarding earlier decisions, those can be readily reconsidered. Only as consultation is made the organizing principle of every project can the efforts and commitment of the participants be effective.

> No man can attain his true station except through his justice. No power can exist except through unity. No welfare and no well-being can be attained except through consultation.[335]

---

tion/2#272517715

335 Bahá'u'lláh, quoted in Bahá'u'lláh, 'Abdu'l-Bahá, Shoghi Effendi, Consultation, available at: https://www.bahai.org/library/authoritative-texts/compilations/consultation/2#272517715

Universal Education

The tasks required for development of a global society call for levels of capacity beyond anything humanity has ever mustered. Reaching such levels will require an enormous expansion in access to knowledge, making universal education an indispensable contributor to the process of capacity building. The effort will only succeed, however, when human affairs are reorganized so individuals and groups in every sector of society can easily acquire knowledge and apply it to the shaping of human affairs.

Science and Religion

Throughout recorded history, human consciousness has depended upon two basic spheres of knowledge—science and religion. Through these two domains, often seen as adversaries, humanity's experience has been organized, its environment interpreted, its latent powers explored, and its moral and intellectual life disciplined. These two spheres of knowledge and exploration have acted as the true precursors of civilization. The effectiveness of this dual structure of knowledge has been greatest during those periods when religion and science were able to work in concert.

In the context of a strategy of social and economic development, the relevant issue is how scientific and technological activity is to be organized. If the science involved is viewed chiefly as the preserve of established elites in a few nations, the enormous gap that such an arrangement has already created between the world's rich and poor will only continue to widen with disastrous consequences for the world's economy. If most of the world's citizens are regarded mainly as users of science and technology products created elsewhere, then development programs ostensibly designed to serve their needs cannot properly be termed "development." A better category name might be "marketing."

An enormous challenge, then, is the expansion of scientific and technological activity to more people in more places. Scientific and technological instruments of social and economic change are so powerful they must cease to be the benefactors only of advantaged segments of society. They must be organized to permit participation in such development activity on the basis of capacity. Such reorganization will require viable centers of learning throughout the world to enhance the capability of the world's vast population to generate and apply scientific knowledge. Familiar arguments for maintaining the educational status quo grow less compelling daily as the accelerating revolution in communication technologies brings information and training within reach of people around the globe whatever their cultural backgrounds.

Religious Life

The challenges facing humanity in its religious life are equally daunting. For most of the population, the idea that human nature has a spiritual dimension—that its fundamental identity is spiritual—requires no proof. It is a perception of reality discovered in the earliest records of civilization and has been cultivated for millennia by each of the great wisdom traditions. Its enduring contributions to law, the fine arts and the civilizing of human discourse have given substance and meaning to history. In one form or another, its promptings have a daily influence in the lives of most people on earth, and as current events dramatically show, the longings it awakens are both potent and inextinguishable.

It would seem wise, then, that efforts to promote human progress would seek to tap capacities so universal and immensely creative. Why, then, have spiritual issues facing humanity not been central to the development discourse? Why have most of the priorities and underlying assumptions of international development been determined by materialistic worldviews to which only small minorities of the earth's population subscribe? How much weight can be placed on a professed devotion to universal participation when the validity of the participants' defining cultural experience is ignored?

It may be argued that spiritual and moral issues have historically been kept outside the framework of the international community's development concerns. To accord them any significant role would be to open the door to the dogmatic religious influences that have nurtured social conflict and blocked human progress. Certainly, exponents of the world's many theological systems bear heavy responsibility for the disrepute into which faith has fallen and for the many inhibitions and distortions of spiritual meaning they have fostered.

A more likely answer, however, lies in society's perennial discouragement of the investigation of spiritual reality and the ignoring of the deepest roots of human motivation. To the degree that such censorship has been achieved, the sole effect has been to deliver the shaping of humanity's future into the hands of a new orthodoxy, one which argues that truth is amoral and facts are independent of values.

Many of the greatest achievements of religion, however, have been moral in character. Through its teachings, and through the examples of human lives illumined by these teachings, masses of people have developed the capacity to love. They have learned to discipline the animal side of their natures; to make great sacrifices for the common good; to practice forgiveness, generosity, and trust; to use wealth and other resources in ways that serve the advancement of civilization. Institutional systems have been devised to implant these moral advances into social life on a vast scale.

Previous wisdom traditions eventually become obscured and diverted by sectarian conflict notwithstanding the spiritual impulses released by such transcendent figures as Krishna, Moses, Buddha, Zoroaster, Jesus and Muhammad. In this age, Bahá'u'lláh is renewing the importance of personal virtue and instilling new principles for a unified global society.

The Harmony of Science and Religion

If the challenge is how to empower humankind through a vast increase in access to knowledge, the best strategy must be constructed around an intensifying dialogue between science and religion. In every sphere of human activity, and at every level, the insights and skills that represent scientific accomplishment must look to the force of spiritual commitment and moral principle to ensure their appropriate application. For example, people need to learn how to separate fact from conjecture and to distinguish between subjective views and objective reality. The extent to which individuals and institutions with knowledge to share can contribute to human progress, then, will be determined by their devotion to truth and their detachment from their own interests and passions.

Science must also help people think in terms of process—scientific process and historic process. But for this intellectual advancement to contribute to social and economic development, its perspective must be unclouded by prejudices of race, culture, gender or sectarian belief. Similarly, the training that can enable Earth's inhabitants to learn how to create wealth will advance the aims of development only as that knowledge is illumined by the recognition that service to humankind is the purpose of life and social organization.

As the experience of recent decades has demonstrated, material benefits and endeavors cannot be regarded as ends in themselves. Their value consists not only in providing for humanity's basic needs in housing, food, health care and the like, but in extending the reach of human abilities. In development programs, the most important role of economic efforts is to equip people and institutions with the means through which they can achieve the real purpose of development—laying foundations for a new social order that can cultivate the limitless potentialities latent in human consciousness.

The challenge to economic thinking is to accept this purpose as the motivating force in fostering the creation of means. Only in this way can economics and the related sciences free themselves from the undertow of the materialistic preoccupations that now distract them.

Nowhere is the need for a rigorous dialogue between the work of science and the insights of religion more apparent.

The problem of poverty is a case in point. Proposals aimed at addressing poverty assume that material resources exist or can be created by scientific and technological endeavor. The existence of material resources, then, is seen as a solution that will alleviate and eventually eradicate poverty. Such relief, however, is often not achieved because the necessary scientific and technological advances usually respond to material priorities that are only peripherally related to the real interests of humankind. A radical reordering of these priorities must occur if the burden of poverty is to be finally lifted from the world.

Religion will be severely hampered in contributing to this joint undertaking so long as it is held prisoner by sectarian doctrines that cannot distinguish between contentment and mere passivity, and teach that poverty is an inherent feature of earthly life with only one solution—the world beyond. To participate effectively in the struggle to bring material well-being to humanity, the religious spirit must find new spiritual concepts and principles relevant to an age that seeks to establish unity and justice in human affairs.

Unemployment raises similar issues. In most contemporary thinking, the concept of work is limited to gainful employment to pay for the consumption of available goods. The system is circular—acquisition and consumption results in greater production of goods, which in turn supports paid employment. Each of these activities, of course, are essential to the well-being of society. But the overall concept is inadequate, as can be seen in the apathy and demoralization of workers as reported by social commentators who study such things.

Not surprisingly, then, the world is in urgent need of a new "work ethic." Here again, nothing less than insights from the creative interaction of science and religion can produce fundamental reorientation of habits and attitudes. Unlike animals, which depend for sustenance on whatever the environment provides, human beings express the immense capacities latent within them through productive work that provides the means for sustenance. Through these actions, workers become participants—at however modest a level—in the advancement of civilization. They fulfill purposes that unite them with others.

To the extent that work is consciously performed in a spirit of service to humanity, our latest wisdom tradition tells us it is a form of worship.[336] No narrower perspective will ever call up the magnitude of effort and commitment required by the economic tasks ahead.

Environmental and Global Pressures

As a result of the environmental crisis, a similar challenge faces economic thinking. The fallacy that there is no limit to nature's capacity to fulfill any demand on it has now been coldly exposed. A culture that prizes expansion, acquisition and the satisfaction of people's wants over needs is being compelled to recognize that material goals are not, by themselves, realistic guides to policy. Inadequate, too, are approaches to economic issues where the decision-making tools cannot deal with global challenges.

Until recently, the capacity for contentment, moral discipline and devotion to duty were considered essential aspects of being human. Throughout history, the Teachings of the Founders of our great wisdom traditions have instilled these qualities of character in the peoples of the world. These qualities are even more vital today, but their expression must now take a form consistent with humanity's coming-of-age. Here again, religion's challenge is to free itself from the obsessions of the past. Contentment is not fatalism. Morality has nothing in common with the life-denying puritanism that has so often spoken in its name. A genuine devotion to duty brings feelings not of self-righteousness, as some have feared, but of self-worth.

---

336 'Abdu'l-Bahá, *Paris Talks*.

Equality of Women and Men

The effect of the persistent denial of women's full equality with men sharpens further the challenge to science and religion in the economic life of humankind. The principle of the equality of the sexes represents a truth about human nature that has been largely unrecognized throughout humanity's long childhood and adolescence.

> Women and men have been and will always be equal in the sight of God.[337]

The rational soul has no sex, and whatever social inequities may have been dictated by survival requirements of the past cannot be justified at a time when humanity approaches its coming of age. A commitment to the establishment of full equality between men and women will be central to the success of efforts to conceive and implement a strategy of global development.

Progress in gender equality will itself be a measure of the success of any development program. The challenge goes beyond ensuring an equitable distribution of opportunity. It calls for a fundamental rethinking of economic issues in a manner that will invite women to have participation in the full range of human experience and insight that has been withheld until now.

An Ever-Advancing Civilization

To contemplate a transformation of society on this scale is to question the power that can be harnessed to accomplish it and the authority to exercise that power. As with all other implications of the planet's accelerating integration, both familiar concepts stand in urgent need of redefinition.

---

337 Bahá'u'lláh, quoted in Bahá'u'lláh, 'Abdu'l-Bahá, Shoghi Effendi, *Women*.

Attributes of Power

Despite theological or ideological assurances to the contrary, power historically has been interpreted as advantage enjoyed by certain persons or groups. Often, it has been expressed simply in terms of a means that can be used against others. This interpretation has become a feature of the culture of division and conflict that has characterized humanity during the past several millennia regardless of which social, religious, or political orientations were ascendant anywhere at any given time. In general, power has been an attribute of individuals, factions, peoples, classes and nations. It has been an attribute especially associated with men rather than women. Its chief effect has been to confer on its beneficiaries the ability to acquire, to surpass, to dominate, to resist, to win.

The historical processes resulting from power have been responsible for both ruinous setbacks and extraordinary advances in civilization. To appreciate the benefits is to acknowledge also the setbacks as well as the clear limitations of the behavioral patterns that have produced both. Habits and attitudes related to the use of power have finally reached the outer limits of their effectiveness. In an era with pressing global problems, the archaic notion that power means advantage for segments of humanity is a profoundly mistaken theory of no practical service to the social and economic development of the planet. Those who still adhere to it—and in earlier eras would have felt confident in their adherence—now find their plans enmeshed in inexplicable frustrations and hindrances. In its traditional and competitive meaning, power is as irrelevant to the needs of humanity's future as would be the technologies of railway locomotion to the task of lifting satellites into orbit.

The analogy is apt. By the requirements of its own coming of age, humankind is being urged to free itself from its inherited understanding and uses of power. Humanity has always been able to conceive of power in other forms critical to its hopes. History provides ample evidence that, however intermittently and ineptly, people everywhere and of every background have tapped a wide range of creative resources within themselves. The most obvious example, perhaps, has been the power of truth itself, which is an agent of change associated with some of the greatest advances in the philosophical, religious, artistic, and scientific experience of humankind. Force of character represents another means of mobilizing immense human response, as does the influence of example, whether in the lives of individual human beings or in human societies.

Almost wholly unappreciated is the magnitude of the force that will be generated by the achievement of unity.

> So powerful is the light of unity that it can illuminate the whole earth.[338]

Eventually, the institutions of society will yield authority to principles that are in harmony with the evolving interests of a maturing human race. Such principles include the obligation of those in authority to win the confidence and support of those who they seek to govern; to consult openly and fully with all whose interests are affected by decisions; to assess objectively the genuine needs and aspirations of the communities they serve; and to benefit from scientific and moral advancement so they can make appropriate use of the community's resources. Most importantly, those in authority must give priority to building and maintaining unity among the members of society and its institutions.

Clearly, such principles can operate only within a culture that is democratic in spirit and method. This does not endorse, however, the ideology of partisanship that has boldly usurped democracy's name and today finds itself mired in cynicism, apathy and corruption.

---

338 Bahá'u'lláh, *Gleanings from the Writings of Bahá'u'lláh*..

Coming of Age

Only if humanity's collective childhood has indeed come to an end and its coming of age is dawning does the prospect of an ever-advancing society represent more than another utopian mirage. To imagine that an effort of such magnitude can be summoned up by despondent and mutually antagonistic peoples and nations runs counter to all received wisdom. Only if the course of social evolution has arrived at a decisive turning point through which all of existence is impelled suddenly forward into new stages of development can such a possibility be conceived.

A profound conviction that just so great a transformation in human consciousness is underway has inspired the views set forth in the following statement. To all who recognize in it familiar promptings from within their own hearts, these words from our latest wisdom tradition bring assurance that God has, in this matchless day, endowed humanity with spiritual resources fully equal to the challenge:

> O ye that inhabit the heavens and the earth! There hath appeared what hath never previously appeared. This is the Day in which God's most excellent favors have been poured out upon men, the Day in which His most mighty grace hath been infused into all created things.[339]

> The first sign of the coming of age of humanity referred to in the Writings of Bahá'u'lláh is the emergence of a science which is described as that "divine philosophy" which will include the discovery of a radical approach to the transmutation of elements. This is an indication of the splendours of the future stupendous expansion of knowledge.[340]

---

339 Bahá'u'lláh, *Gleanings from the Writings of Bahá'u'lláh*.
340 Bahá'u'lláh, *The Kitáb-i-Aqdas*, p. 250

> The ages of its infancy and childhood are past, never again to return, while the Great Age, the consummation of all ages, which must signalize the coming of age of the entire human race, is yet to come. The convulsions of this transitional and most turbulent period in the annals of humanity are the essential prerequisites, and herald the inevitable approach, of that Age of Ages, "the time of the end," in which the folly and tumult of strife that has, since the dawn of history, blackened the annals of mankind, will have been finally transmuted into the wisdom and the tranquility of an undisturbed, a universal, and lasting peace, in which the discord and separation of the children of men will have given way to the worldwide reconciliation, and the complete unification of the divers elements that constitute human society.[341]

---

341 Shoghi Effendi, *The Promised Day is Come*, p. 117.

Afterword

As humanity has continued its advance toward a modern civilization, new and more complex issues have continued to require new wisdom and principles to live by. A succession of new Divine Educators have appeared to guide humanity in this process, each One offering expanded knowledge and renewed principles, and each promising humankind that another Divine Educator would follow. These Messengers have appeared centuries apart yet each one reflects the rise of the same sun, though They are called by different names as Jesus explained:

> Howbeit when he, the Spirit of truth, is come, he will guide you into all truth: for he shall not speak of himself; but whatsoever he shall hear, that shall he speak: and he will shew you things to come.[342]

This book would not be complete without the following words from Bahá'u'lláh, the most recent Divine Educator, which support the pathway of thinking and understanding proposed in this book:

> O Jews! If ye be intent on crucifying once again Jesus, the Spirit of God, put Me to death, for He hath once more, in My person, been made manifest unto you.

---

342 *The Bible*, John 16:13.

> Deal with Me as ye wish, for I have vowed to lay down My life in the path of God. I will fear no one, though the powers of earth and heaven be leagued against Me.

> Followers of the Gospel! If ye cherish the desire to slay Muhammad, the Apostle of God, seize Me and put an end to My life, for I am He, and My Self is His Self. Do unto Me as ye like, for the deepest longing of Mine heart is to attain the presence of My Best-Beloved in His Kingdom of Glory. Such is the Divine decree, if ye know it.

> Followers of Muhammad! If it be your wish to riddle with your shafts the breast of Him Who hath caused His Book the Bayán to be sent down unto you, lay hands on Me and persecute Me, for I am His Well-Beloved, the revelation of His own Self, though My name be not His name. I have come in the shadows of the clouds of glory, and am invested by God with invincible sovereignty. He, verily, is the Truth, the Knower of things unseen. I, verily, anticipate from you the treatment ye have accorded unto Him that came before Me.

> If ye have resolved to shed the blood of Him... Whose advent Muhammad hath prophesied, and Whose Revelation Jesus Christ Himself hath announced, behold Me standing, ready and defenseless, before you. Deal with Me after your own desires.[343]

---

343 Bahá'u'lláh, *Gleanings from the Writings of Bahá'u'lláh*, pp. 101-102.

Research and Study Sources

For those who want to consult the Bahá'í Writings and the sacred Writings of other wisdom traditions discussed in this book, we recommend the following sources:

Bahá'í Reference Library

The authoritative online source of Bahá'í writings. It contains selected works of Bahá'u'lláh, the Báb, 'Abdu'lBahá, Shoghi Effendi, and the Universal House of Justice, as well as other Bahá'í texts.

https://www.bahai.org/library/

Uplifting Words (Online)

An online list of Bahá'í-only texts in multiple formats for reading or download.

https://www.upliftingwords.org/post/baha-i-sacred-texts

Ocean 2.0 Interfaith Reader

An immersive library of the world's sacred literature. Read or listen to texts from these religions: Hindu, Judaism, Confucian, Tao, Islam, Zoroastrianism, Jainism, Buddhist, Christian, Bahai Faith.

https://sacred-traditions.org/ocean/

The Bahá'í Faith Websites

To learn more about The Bahá'í Faith in the United States, visit:

http://www.bahai.us

To learn more about The Bahá'í Faith worldwide, visit:

https://www.bahai.org/w

Acknowledgements

We must first acknowledge all of the world's great wisdom traditions and those who for millennia have labored to recover, preserve and translate the collective knowledge of the Divine Educators in a form accessible to all humanity. Thanks also to the many advisors and readers of the manuscript who have helped immensely to improve the content and clarity of our prose.

Thanks also to our publishing company, Calumet Editions, and its talented staff for their commitment and long hours correcting our mistakes, improving our language and style, and making sure that our book had no (or few) lapses in logic. The authors appreciate every challenge they gave us.

Thanks also to Sona Hegedus and Marsha Milani for their immense contributions in collating information and helping evaluate the complex manuscript that resulted.

About the Authors

Massoud Kazemzadeh, PhD

Dr. Kazemzadeh holds a PhD in food engineering from Texas A&M University. This is his second book not related to the field of food production and follows *The Soul of Humanity*. His passion is defining religious scriptures through the lens of science and logical thinking. He is currently working on a third volume about the rationality inherent in the founding principles of the world's great religions. After selling his two food companies, Kay's Naturals and Kay's Processing, he retired to Clara City, Minnesota, where he makes his home with his wife. He has two children and four grandchildren, all of whom live in Minnesota.

Gary Lindberg

Before starting his career in writing and publishing books, Gary Lindberg was an award-winning filmmaker with over a hundred national and international awards. He produced and co-wrote the Paramount feature film *That Was Then, This Is Now* starring Emilio Estevez and Morgan Freeman. Since then, he has authored four #1 bestselling novels and many nonfiction titles. He lives in Minnesota where he has published books for over a hundred authors with his partner at Calumet Editions, Ian Graham Leask.

www.ingramcontent.com/pod-product-compliance
Lightning Source LLC
Chambersburg PA
CBHW020743100426
42735CB00037B/327